LIKE LIVING STONES

The Ray S. Anderson Collection

Ray Sherman Anderson (1925–2009) worked the soil and tended the animals of a South Dakota farm, planted and pastored a church in Southern California, and completed a PhD degree in theology with Thomas F. Torrance in New College Edinburgh. He began his professional teaching career at Westmont College, and then taught and served in various administrative capacities at Fuller Theological Seminary for thirty-three years (retiring as Professor Emeritus of Theology and Ministry). While teaching at Fuller, he served as a parish pastor, always insisting that theology and ministry go hand-in-hand.

The pastoral theologian who began his teaching career in middle age penned twenty-seven books. Like Karl Barth, Prof. Anderson articulated a theology of and for the church based on God's own ministry of revelation and reconciliation in the world. As professor and pastor, he modeled an incarnational, evangelical passion for the healing of humanity by Jesus Christ, who is *both* God's self-revelation to us *and* the reconciliation of our broken humanity to the triune God. His gift of relating suffering and alienated humans to Christ existing as community (Dietrich Bonhoeffer) is a recurrent motif throughout his life, ministry, and works.

The Ray S. Anderson Collection comprises books by Ray Anderson, an introductory text to his theology by Christian D. Kettler, two edited volumes that celebrate his distinguished academic career (*Incarnational Ministry: The Presence of Christ in Church, Society, and Family* and *On Being Christian . . . and Human*), and a reprint of an Edification volume that focuses on Ray Anderson's contributions to the field of Christian Psychology. A word of gratitude is due to The Society of Christian Psychology and its parent organization, The American Association for Christian Counselors, for their permission to make the *Edification* issue available in book form. Jim Tedrick of Wipf and Stock Publishers deserves a special word of thanks for publishing many of Ray Anderson's books and commissioning this collection of works to continue his legacy.

Todd H. Speidell, General Editor

LIKE LIVING STONES

A series of messages based on
the Statement of Faith of the
Evangelical Free Church of America

by

Ray S. Anderson

WIPF & STOCK · Eugene, Oregon

Wipf and Stock Publishers
199 W 8th Ave, Suite 3
Eugene, OR 97401

Like Living Stones
By Anderson, Ray S. and Olson, Arnold T.
Copyright©1964 by Anderson, Ray S.
ISBN 13: 978-1-60899-619-3
Publication date 4/12/2010
Previously published by Free Church Press,
Minneapolis, Minnesota, 1964

*Gratefully dedicated to the
members and friends of
the Covina Evangelical Free Church.
Their Lives are . . .*
LIVING STONES

PREFACE

It has long been my conviction that preaching includes both content and encounter. The occasion of a sermon is more than delivery of what has been prepared. It is the encountering of God through the proclamation of the Word that quickens the hearts of both speaker and listener in such a way that what is said becomes secondary to what transpires. If what is said becomes the occasion for a moment of truth, the individual can never again be the same—whether he speaks or listens.

Thus it is with some reluctance that these messages are presented to be read out of the context of the original encounter. The written word has a different purpose than the spoken word. Nevertheless, the deed is done! Here they are for what they are. The messages were tape-recorded at the time of their presentation. If they appear to be informal in places and unpolished in style, it is because they were not re-written in any way, but simply transcribed for publication with a minimum of editing to increase readability and retain as far as possible the expressions of the spoken word. It is my secret hope that the reader will occasionally be carried beyond the content into the moment of communication itself. It is this possibility of response that justifies the endeavor.

During the spring and summer of 1963, I presented a series of messages based on the twelve-point Statement of Faith accepted by the Evangelical Free Church of America at the merger conference in 1950. My purpose was two-fold: first, to involve our constituency in the distinctives of the Evangelical Free Church through an understanding of the Statement of Faith. But more important, to bring the great redemptive truths of God's Word into living expression through committed lives. A statement of faith is not meant to be the test of orthodoxy when applied to individual lives, but rather the affirmations of those who have experienced redemptive love. The experiencing of redemption is always a greater reality than the definitions of that experience. These twelve points are not pillars upon which the church is built, but voices from the church itself, speaking in unison of common faith. The words of Peter reflect this dynamic truth, "Come to him, to that living stone . . . and like living stones be yourselves built into a spiritual house . . .". (I Peter 2:4-5)* *Like living stones,* our lives build the edifice that Christ called His Church. Through these messages it was my prayer that the truth of what *We Believe* would come alive through the response of faith.

It must be understood that these messages do not represent the official position of the Evangelical Free Church of America. Indeed, if the chapters on The Church are read, it will be readily apparent that this would be impossible even if it were my intent! The Evangelical Free Church is not one voice, but one people who all speak with the same authority of their mutual faith.

Nevertheless, I speak as a minister of the Evangelical Free Church and raise my voice from within this fellowship.

These words belong to the Evangelical Free Church by my conviction that they are true to the spirit and distinctives which we cherish as Biblical and historical. Not all will agree with my interpretations of these truths, nor would all of my colleagues share the same convictions. I trust, however, that all will read in the spirit that I have spoken—a desire not to prove but to involve; an obligation not to defend but to inspire. That this inspiration may lead to incarnation of truth itself—like living stones.

A special word of acknowledgment is due Mrs. Evelyn Iverson for her painstaking labor of transcribing and preparing the manuscript, and for her inspiration and assistance in undertaking the project.

Covina, California   Ray S. Anderson
June, 1964

* All Scripture quotations are from the Revised Standard Version.

INTRODUCTION

Doctrinal statements and church creeds generally make tedious reading. While they do inform, they do not often inspire. Attempts to clarify them ofttimes add to their complications and detract from their appeal. While many sermons have been preached and books written on the great creeds of Christendom, few have attempted to present them as bases for devotional studies.

The author is to be commended for venturing into this field, which to one who has spent many years interpreting the twelve articles of our faith has become an adventure. When first told what he had endeavored to accomplish, I wondered what he might add to that which had already been said and written. The manuscript soon revealed that he had made and was sharing some most delightful discoveries.

While this volume is not an official interpretation of the doctrinal position of our church, it nevertheless is a valuable contribution to the increasing number of volumes on the subject. While his application of the statements to everyday life are the results of his own study and meditation, they nevertheless will bring a response especially to those familiar with the creed. While one does not expect complete agreement with any personal conclusion in this area, for differences of opinion within the broad framework of our creedal declarations are not only permitted but encouraged, the reader will agree that the author has caught the spirit of the statement. It has been said that certain facts are not "taugh but caugh." In this instance they are both taught and caught.

These pages offer hours of pleasant reading and many inspiring thoughts for meditation. Truly the foundation stones become living stones on its pages.

Arnold T. Olson

CONTENTS

Chapter		Page
1	THE WORD WE CHERISH	13
2	THE GOD WE WORSHIP	23
3	THE CHRIST WE SERVE	32
4	THE SPIRIT WE KNOW	42
5	THE HUMAN PREDICAMENT	52
6	THE DIVINE ENABLEMENT	61
7	THE SYMBOLS OF LOVE	71
8	THE CHURCH — A BELIEVING COMMUNITY	80
9	THE CHURCH — A COMMITTED COMMUNITY	90
10	THE CHURCH — A DISCIPLINED COMMUNITY	99
11	OUR BLESSED HOPE	109
12	OUR GLORIOUS HERITAGE	119

ARTICLE I

We believe the Scriptures, both Old and New Testaments, to be the inspired Word of God, without error in the original writings, the complete revelation of His will for the salvation of men, and the Divine and final authority for all Christian faith and life.

CHAPTER ONE

THE WORD WE CHERISH

It is significant that a Statement of Faith begins with an affirmation of God's Word, and one reason for this is that it is through God's Word that all knowledge of God is derived. The truth is that when we reduce all of the distinctions and differences in Christendom we come to the irreducible minimum of God's Word. I have always discovered that in entering into dialogue with any type of religious belief and any form of Christianity the concept of God's Word is the determining factor. This is not always readily apparent; but when it comes right down to the essential basis, it is one's concept of Scripture that determines the entire dimension of faith and of the church.

This is why it is important for us to understand that God's Word is not a matter of indifference. Our faith is not dependent upon the assurance that we have within our hearts, but it is dependent upon the authority of the Word of God which witnesses to our hearts. For it is God who speaks to us of what is true; and if this book is simply the record of man who has somehow devised a theology, no matter how well worked out it is, it doesn't make much difference—because who would dare to believe it? I can come to you and tell you your sins are forgiven and it wouldn't make a great deal of difference, because it's not enough to be able to say the words—your sins are forgiven. The important thing is that God said it. If He hasn't said it, nothing that man says can really be definitive about sin. If He has said it, then this becomes the authority for all of man's experience.

The first question we need to ask it—what IS the Bible? And this is not as facetious as it sounds. What IS the Bible? The best seller? Nine million copies sold last year, and yet perhaps the least read of all best sellers: What IS the Bible? What does it mean to you? A memento of former days in Sunday School? A personal possession carried in your pocket as some kind of a good luck charm? Is the Bible a mystery book, so mysterious and wonderful that if you happen to open it up and read a verse, this is supposed to bring about almost a magical effect? Is this what the Bible is to you?

Now there is in our Statement of Faith a key word concerning the Bible. If you will look about halfway through the Statement, you will find that it states that the Bible is the complete revelation of God's will. Now have we helped ourselves very much—do we know what revelation is? That which is revealed is that which can be discovered about someone or something else, not through observation but from revelation from the other—so that revelation is more than discovery. The scientist makes discoveries, but he does not look for revelations. He does not look for that which he studies to speak to him. He observes, he watches, he measures, he interprets, he photographs, he probes, and in all of the probing and studying he discovers a lot of things about that which he studies.

One key use of the word "revelation" brings its dynamic meaning more clearly to us when we think about revelation between persons. Here is a stranger. Now there are certain things that can be discovered about a stranger—you can measure him; you know he is so many feet and so many inches tall. You can weigh him and know how many pounds and ounces he weighs. You can watch him and observe certain characteristics of his personality. You can observe him, and you can begin to make moral judgments as to whether he is a good or a bad man; and if you are careful, you can compile quite a file on your observations of who that man is and what he's like. But none of this is revelation in its most dynamic form because there is so much *he* controls and *he* must reveal. When he begins to speak, then he begins to reveal, and the revelation of who that man is is what he reveals of himself, not what we can simply discover.

Now then, the word "revelation" is much more than what we have discovered about God—it is what God has chosen to give to us concerning Himself; and if we use the word "revelation" in that sense, we will have a wonderful key to what the Bible is. The Bible is that which God has chosen to make known to us concerning Himself which we could never have discovered in any other way. One marvelous thing about the Bible is that it does not duplicate human ingenuity. The Bible does not pretend to be a short cut to human knowledge, and if you want to be a good scientist and discover a lot of things about the laws of life, you are not going to find them in the Bible because the Bible is a book of revelation, not of discovery. The Bible speaks to us of those things concerning God that could never have been discovered, and this bears true in every field of human endeavor, whether it's science, psychology or philosophy. Wherever you find God's Word speaking, it will not be in contradiction to that which is discovered of truth, nor will it be a substitute for good discovery itself. There is a harmony between that which God reveals and that which man discovers, and the two are compatible.

There are two forms of revelation. We speak of God revealing Himself in His creation, and the very handiwork of God is a testimony as to who God is. God has spoken to us when He created the world because He created certain things that are revealing of who God is. Do we not have a right to say that the beauty of nature is a revelation of God's beauty, that the harmony of the world is an evidence of God's nature, and that in the majesty and the infinity of the creation, there is a revealing of the infinity of God Himself, without beginning or end?

The second form of revelation is special revelation, and to the word "revelation" we must now add another word, and that word is "redemption." Now redemption is simply the movement of God towards man who is a sinner, and redemption and special revelation are linked together. Whenever God acts, it is part of His redeeming revelation. The Scripture sets the stage in the very opening scene of mankind. We have the fall of man, and then God seeks man and says, "Adam, where art thou?" This is an activity on the part of God seeking man, and it is rightly called redemption. The Bible is the book of God's redemptive revelation. It is the seeking of man and the story of finding him.

There are two things involved with God's redemptive activity: first of all, the act in which God does something, and then the interpretation of the act. The Bible is the record of God's redemptive acting in history and the interpretation of it—the two together comprise Scripture. We will illustrate this. In I Cor. 15:3 Paul speaks of the gospel, and here is what he says —Christ died. Now this is no mystery. This could be seen and observed by those who were there, and if you could have stood before Calvary on that afternoon when Christ was crucified, you would have seen three men die and you would have known that one of them was Jesus Christ. This is a fact. But Scripture is more than just objective fact. Christ died, Paul says, for our sins—and thus the meaning of that death is not simply that He died but that He died in behalf of man's sin, and until we have the interpretation of that death, we have no meaning to it. If a stranger should walk into this room and without saying a word should walk up to the piano and play three chords and then walk up and hand me a note and leave without saying a word, you would have seen something but you would have no knowledge of what went on. Only when that note was read would you know he purpose of it.

Herein is involved the problem of Scripture. Who has a right to say what the death of Christ means? Paul said—Christ died for our sins. Suppose I should say—well, He died as an example of a good man fighting a lost cause. Now which is right—don't I have a right to my opinion? If Paul has his opinion, I have mine. Why does Paul's word become Scripture, and what I say has to be corrected by what Paul says? Here we are involved with what Scripture is. The Word of God speaks with divine authority, not only of the fact, but of the interpretation of the fact; and when Paul says—Christ died for our sins—he is not simply giving us an opinion. He was saying—this is what God has revealed to me, and the truth of this is because God has said it.

You will note in our Statement of Faith we have used the word "inspiration"—God's Word is inspired. We have to be sure that God said it; if God said it, it is true. Our only problem is—did God say it? So now we must move into the realm of not only what IS the Bible, but is the Bible true? How do we know that when Paul said—Christ died for our sins—this is a true interpretation? If you will follow me carefully for a few moments, I am going to show you what the Bible claims for itself. We must understand this, and if we can show very clearly and briefly what the Bible claims for itself, then the Bible can be judged to be either true or false in what it claims.

First of all, the phrase or its equivalent, "Thus saith the Lord" is used over 2000 times in the Old Testament. This would speak to us very clearly of the fact that the Old Testament conveys to us the impression that it is God speaking and not man. The Old Testament does not in any place suggest that these words are contrived by human ingenuity, but "thus saith the Lord." Now the second step—the New Testament claims that the Old Testament was inspired of God. "All Scripture is inspired by God" (II Tim. 3:16). Now the Scripture in possession at the time this was written was the Old Testament. I need not remind you that the new Testament was not written yet—it was being written—so that when Paul in II Timothy uses the word "Scripture" he is referring to the Old Testament, and he says of the Old Testament, "All Scripture is inspired of God."

The Greek word for "inspiration" is literally "God-breathed." Scripture has been breathed out by God, spoken by God. "No prophecy ever came by the impulse of man, but men moved by the Holy Spirit spoke from God" (II Peter 1:21). "God spoke through the prophets of old" (Heb. 1:1). The New Tesatment claims that the Old Testament was inspired.

Now we must move to the New Testament itself. How do we know that it is true? Well, the New Testament authors claimed divine authority for what they wrote, and this can be very quickly shown. There was a self-consciousness on the part of the authors of the New Testament that they were writing inspired words. In I Cor. 2:13 Paul says, "We impart this in words not taught by human wisdom, but taught by the Spirit." Paul says—our words are not due to human wisdom but are taught of the Holy Spirit. In I Cor. 14:37 in the midst of a rather practical dissertation Paul pauses to remind them, "If anyone thinks that he is a prophet or spiritual, he shoud acknowledge that what I am writing to you is a command of the Lord." He had this self-consciousness that what he was saying had been commanded of God. In II Cor. 13 we have a further development of this thought. Verse 3, "Since you desire proof that Christ is speaking in me . . ." In other words, the words that I speak is a speaking of Christ. "And we also thank God constantly for this that when you received the word of God which you heard from us, you accepted it not as the word of man but as it really is, the word of God, which is at work in you believers" (I Thess. 2:13). Could anything be plainer than this—Paul says that not only do *we* think that what we speak is the inspired word of God, but we thank God that when we spoke it *you* accepted it, not as our word but as the very word of God. At least we have to say this, that the New Testament authors conceived of their authorship as being divinely inspired. If it were not, they were mistaken, but at least we know what the claim is.

One other thought—Jesus promised His disciples they would be preserved from error through the Holy Spirit. In John 16:13 speaking of the Holy Spirit, Jesus said, "When the spirit of truth comes, he will guide you into all the truth; for he will not speak on his own authority, but whatever he hears he will speak, and he will declare to you the things that are to come." Jesus promised that the disciples, writing of future things, would be preserved from error through the Holy Spirit. Do we not then have a right to say the Bible claims for itself to be the Word of God, not human wisdom, but divinely inspired. If we wish to accept this premise, we accept this to be the very Word of God. If we refuse this premise, we have to also accept the fact that the authors themselves were deceived, and I ask only this of the person who says that the Bible is not a divine book—I ask him to treat it then as less than human, but don't confuse the issue. Don't try to speak of this book as the finest of human writing when it is contrived on a fallacy. Be honest with yourself—either God wrote it, or it is less than human because these men were deceived and deceivers. How easy it is for us to deceive ourselves by thinking we can evade the implications of what God says and can take what we like out of it and accept that. Be honest with Scripture—it is either what it claims to be, or it's not worth our time.

Why is the Bible important to us—why do we cherish this Word? We cherish this Word because it *cleanses the heart*. In Psalm 119, the longest of the Psalms, the wonderful Psalm that speaks of the Word of God in so many different ways, verse 9 says, "How can a young man keep his way pure, by guarding it according to thy word. With my whole heart I seek thee; let me not wander from thy commandments. I have laid up thy word in my heart, that I might not sin against thee." We cherish this Word because it cleanses the heart. Do you know how it cleanses the heart? If you read it, it will mirror your heart. If you read God's Word and come to it as God's Word, your heart shall be viewed for what it is, and God's Word shall carefully define the sin in your heart; and when sin has been defined it can be dealt with, and the evasiveness of your life shall be clarified by the sharpness of God's Word. Jesus said—do not mistake your life, that which comes out of your heart defiles you. And the Word of God purifies the heart. Jesus said to His disciples—now you are clean through the Word which I have spoken unto you. We cherish the Word because it is the place of cleansing;; it is the place of clarification of the moral and spiritual nature of our life.

We cherish this Word because it is an *illumination for our way*. In the same Psalm 119, verse 105: "Thy Word is a lamp to my feet and a light to my path." We cherish this Word because it speaks to us of infallible moral and spiritual principles. We would not pretend for a moment that this book will help you in the working out of your budget or in decisions of a practical nature from the standpoint of simply reading answers. There is no place in God's Word where you are able to read easy answers to a difficult life; but if you are confused and wandering, if somehow in the midst of your life you are not sure of direction, you come to God's Word and you will be infallibly steered to moral and spiritual truth. It's a lamp to our path. I have counseled with many people who have been utterly discouraged and confused and have not known which way to turn, and when we have simply turned to God's Word, there has been an almost instantaneous insight and the response is—now I see, how could I have been so blind, now it's clear, this is the right thing to do. We cherish the Word because it enlightens our path and gives us direction.

We cherish the Word because it is an *anchor for the soul*. In Hebrews 6 we have the very finest statement of what the Word of God can mean to the human heart. The author of Hebrews is speaking of the unchangeable purpose of God revealed through His own oath and His own person, and in verse 19 he says, "We have this as a sure and steadfast anchor of the soul." The one thing that our age needs is an anchor for the soul. It almost makes one sick to look around at the desperateness with which many are trying to find spiritual answers, to look upon the philosophies that are offered men, to look upon the answers that are passed out as if there were messiahs around every corner. Where shall a man or a woman turn today for an anchor, for something that is true, for something that will not ultimately lead to disgust or disillusionment? There is no other place to turn but to what God has said.

Most of you, because most of you are young, have not found it sufficient yet to have an anchor. You don't need it. Most of you can buy almost everything you need. Very few of you have stood poised at the edge of a grave and have read back to your hearts your own philosophy of life. Very few of you have had to put your life to the test; very few of you have had to take your life for what it has been the past week and lay it on the line and say—it is worth it. So most of you have plenty of time to try a lot of things. But I have stood at the graveside, and I have stood there with the recognition that there isn't another book in the world worth reading, there isn't poem, there isn't a bit of philosophy, there isn't a phrase no matter how well turned, that is worth reading at the grave, because the grave speaks to us of ultimate realities of life and death and sin and resurrection, and the Word of God alone is an anchor for the soul. "I am the resurrection and the life, he that believes in me, though he die, yet shall he live, and whoever lives and believes in me shall never die. In my Father's house are many rooms; if it were not so, would I have told you that I go to prepare a place for you? If we confess our sins, he is faithful and just and will forgive our sins and cleanse us from all unrighteousness. And I saw a new heaven, and a new earth . . . the holy city . . . coming down out of heaven from God" (John 11:25-26, 14:2, I John 1:9, Rev. 21:1-2). And in that city there is no more weeping, no more sorrow, no more failure, no more death, no more disease, for all these things are passed away, and that city has no need of a sun because the Son of God lights the city. Yes—this is an anchor for the soul, isn't it—and you'll need it sooner or later.

I've also stood at gravesides and have had nothing to say though I had the Word in my hands; I've had nothing to say because the one in the grave had no response in life. He had no use for this in his life and had no reason to hear it at his death. The Word of God is only a comfort to that soul which has cast its own peace and security upon the Word. If it's true today, it's a sufficient anchor for the human soul. And if it's true and you are in disobedience to it, this same Word shall have to be read, and this Word says that there will be a resurrection of the unjust as well as the just and that a man's deeds will follow him. Is that true—does your sin follow you, or do you leave it on the pillow where you weep? Ah, it is true. We cherish the Word—we cherish the Word because it is not just an infallible record of truth, but because God has spoken so that man may believe and receive. "My words," said Jesus, "are words of life and truth. I am the way, the truth, and the life. No man comes to the Father, but by me." We cherish this Word because God has spoken—and we have answered.

ARTICLE II

We believe in one God, Creator of all things, infinitely perfect and eternally existing in three persons, Father, Son, and Holy Spirit.

CHAPTER TWO

THE GOD WE WORSHIP

The storm of atheism has not yet reached us. We have felt only the first cold gusts of its approach. Our age lives in the shadow of another generation's faith. We use the vocabulary of another age which believed in a personal God. The ethics of our society are left-over Christian ethics of another age vaguely carried along because somehow they belong to our age but without a positive basis in a personal relationship to a personal God.

In a recent survey taken at a large university it was discovered that college and university students when asked the simple question—do you believe in God?—responded in the affirmative. Ninety-seven out of a hundred answered the question—yes—and only 3% would at that point acknowledge that they absolutely did not believe in God. On the same questionnaire another question was asked—if you believe in God, do you pray?—and over 60% of the college and university students who believed in God said—yes, they had at least some form of prayer that they had prayed to their God. On the same questionnaire another question was asked—do you have a deep and personal assurance that you know God—and less than 10% answered in the affirmative, so that even out of the 97% who claimed to believe in God less than 10% had any deep and personal assurance that they knew God. So we ought not to be fooled by the professions of belief in God that carry with them a personal agnosticism, because after all the word "agnostic" simply means—I do not know—and how can one believe that there is a God and yet have any assurance of personal salvation if they do not know Him. Could we not ascribe to our present age that which was ascribed to the age of Paul as he spoke on Mars Hill and said—I noticed on the way to this meeting your altar on which you have inscribed "To the unknown god." How long do you think the ethics and vocabulary and lingering faith of another age is going to permeate and continue to have its effect on an age which has only an unknown god?

It is important that we believe in God. I want to convey to you from God's Word who is our God, for agnosticism is insufficient. When we speak of God, automatically our minds stiffen up and we sit straight in our chairs and prepare for an academic and dry lecture on theology. But theology is only the definition of God's experience in human history, and the Word of God is not a textbook on theology but an inspired record of God's revelation of Himself to man. In the revelation of God to man certain things begin to appear concerning who God is. To be very simple, let us begin by discussing from the Word the being of God—who is He? God is a personal being, and He has a name.

Now what would you do if you found a person without a name? If someone doesn't have a name we might give him a number, and perhaps it won't be long before we all have numbers instead of names. But is a number as good as a name? There's nothing very personal about a number, but a name is something else because a name has personality. A name stands for the person we mean when we say Joe or Mary or Mike. We are not saying just a number, we are not saying—hey, you—we are saying all that you are. A name then reveals something, and there was a time names were distributed according to character, or at least hopeful character. We hoped the name might mean that the person would turn out that way.

If you turn to God's Word you will find that the names of the Bible reveal the character of the persons behind them. For instance, the name "Joshua"—Joshua is from the Hebrew word *yasha,* which means in Hebrew "to save" or "to deliver." And the name Joshua means "God saves" or "God delivers." The Greek equivalent in translation of the name "Joshua" is "Jesus" meaning "God saves" or "God delivers" so that in Matthew 1:21 the name was given to Jesus by God Himself because of its meaning "God saves." "Thou shalt call his name Jesus for he shall save his people from their sins."

God always reveals Himself by name. In the opening chapters of Genesis it is "Elohim" who creates heaven and earth. Through this name God is known as One full of majesty, strength, and power.

In the sixth chapter of Exodus God speaks to Moses, "I appeared to Abraham, to Isaac, and to Jacob as God Almighty." Here the name of God is "El Shaddai," which reveals Him to be One who overrules nature to work out His purpose and grace through human history. It is interesting to note in this same context another name by which God reveals Himself. "By my name 'the Lord' I did not make myself known to them" (Exodus 6:3). Here God clearly reveals the progressive sequence through which the names were first known by man. In the third chapter of Exodus this name "the Lord," commonly translated as "Jehovah" is revealed to Moses for the first time in the covenantal terms of redemption. As Jehovah, God is known for His loving concern and covenantal relationship with the people of His choice.

This progressive revealing of God's nature through the history of redemption brings the God of creation into personal relationship with the persons of His creation. As a person, God is encountered in His personality, not His impersonal creation.

Some would make of God a mathematical formula, or a universal cosmic principle. But we read in Psalm 94, "Understand, O dullest of the people! Fools, when will you be wise? He who planted the ear, does he not hear? He who formed the eye, does he not see? He who chastens the nations, does he not chastise? He who teaches men knowledge, the Lord, knows the thoughts of man, that they are but a breath." Here is God reasoning with us and saying—listen, he that made the eye can see, he that made man who can think can think himself, he who made man to feel can feel, he who made man to love can love, and he who made man to breathe can breathe. And so the being of God, the God that we worship, is a God who is a personal being, who feels and hears and sees and loves and is disappointed and is joyful. This is our God—a person, not a mathematical formula, not a thing that can only be discovered, but one who can be known.

In John 4 we have a definition of God. In the story of Jesus speaking to the woman by the Samaritan well Jesus defines God in verse 24 by saying, "God is spirit." Now spirit simply means a personal being without flesh and blood. I am sorry that I cannot show you God today because He has no flesh and blood. I cannot take a human form and say—this is God. When I speak of spirit, you may say I am speaking of some vague thing that has no form at all. A spirit has form, but it has a form of spiritual reality. A person is more than a body; you are more than your body. When you send someone a letter, through that letter a person can share what you have said without ever seeing your body. This is because the real you has communicated itself through the symbols of the words. Now God is a spirit, and God can communicate Himself to us for all the reality that He is even though we cannot now touch Him or feel Him. And yet it was the Jesus who said—God is spirit—who also said—I and the Father are one, and if you've seen me you've seen God. So momentarily God became flesh and blood, that we like children might touch Him in order that we might discover that God is not afraid to be touched but that God is *more* than flesh and blood. The being of God is revealed to be personal. He is a real spiritual being who can be with us as individuals wherever we are.

You will note that the Statement of Faith speaks of one God—"We believe in one God." Now some wise person might say—which one—as if we had selected out of a lot of gods one god and said—this is the only true God. No, we believe that God is one—in other words, we believe in the unity of God, and we will not accept anything less than that God encompasses everything so that there is no thought that we have a God here who is greater than other gods. It's not a matter of choosing between gods—it's a matter of saying that God is everything, that He is one. There is no dualism in God. It's not that God is partly evil and partly good and that the good overcomes evil, that God is partly darkness and partly light and that the light is stronger than the darkness. God is one. And in the oneness of God the unity of His creation exists, and this is why there is harmony in the world and meaning to our life because God is one, and everything that proceeds from God has unity to it, has oneness.

If we could stop there, you would say—I understand, it's very simple. But we have to go on and say—nonetheless, God is three, Father, Son and Holy Spirit. Now if you will momentarily visualize two things and hold one in one hand and one in the other for awhile. In your left hand hold the thought —God is three persons, Father, Son and Holy Spirit. Now you can hold both thoughts. In your left hand you have the thought—God is one—and in the right hand the thought— God is three, Father, Son and Holy Spirit. Now how many persons are you when you are holding this? You are one—so that it's not impossible for you at least as one person to understand and hold both thoughts. Now this is very elementary, but it shows us that at least we are talking about something that has unity. There is no reason to say that it takes two people to hold these two thoughts. If we can as one person hold both thoughts, is it impossible to think that God can be both? If we can hold both thoughts without having to deny one or the other, cannot God who made us *be* both?

This is what I'm going to say about the trinity. First of all, the word "trinity" is not in the Bible, but that's all right—the idea is there. The word "trinity" was coined by a man named Tertullian in about the year 200 A.D. He coined the word to express the relationships which the Bible reveals God has to man, first of all as Father, then as Son, then as Holy Spirit. It is very easy to remember the three persons of the Trinity if you remember it this way: the Father is the one who initiates and creates, the Son is the one who mediates this, who actually is the agent for working it out, so that it is said that God is the Father, the creator, but that the creation took place through the Son who is the Word of God—so the Father initiates, the Son mediates, and the Holy Spirit effectually works to bring it about. For instance, when we speak of redemption, we are speaking of the three phases of God in action. The Father initiates redemption because from the Father's heart love proceeds; the Son mediates redemption because the Son came to die for us on the cross and take our sin upon Himself; the Holy Spirit effectually works redemption because the Holy Spirit enters into our hearts and we are born again. Until this happens, we have not met God, because God is one, and in knowing the Holy Spirit we have met the true God. We believe in one God, Father, Son, and Holy Spirit.

Now let's go on. In the being of God we have His relationship to us as a person, in the unity of God we have the harmony of our life and of the entire creation, in the perfection of God we have the absoluteness of every law and every truth. You will notice in our Statement of Faith we state we believe in God perfect and eternally existing. Infinitely perfect—not that God must pass the test when we judge Him as to whether or not He is just and righteous, but God is infinitely perfect; that is, He is the beginning and the end, and there is nothing outside of that to judge Him by. Whatever God does is righteousness and justice. This is difficult for us because we look at what God does, and we say—that's not fair, it's not right that God should do this. But where do we find this idea of rightness in order to carry it over and apply it to God? He is the beginning and the end. This is found in Isaiah 45, verse 6, "That men may know, from the rising of the sun and from the west, that there is none besides me; I am the Lord, and there is no other. I form light and create darkness, I make weal and create woe, I am the Lord, who do all these things." The Lord is the beginning and the end, and everything that exists in the world has a place in God's providence and in His design, and even the darkness of the world is not outside the scrutiny of God. Do you realize what a comfort this is—to have a God who is infinitely perfect so that there is no evil force, no tragedy of darkness that can occur that is outside of God's control. He is the beginning and the end, and we are circumscribed—our life, our world, and even sin is within the sovereignty of God. He knows the power of sin, and He is a greater power. So it's not just an academic thing to say we believe in God who is infinitely perfect. We are saying we believe in a God who is greater than our sin, who is deeper than our despair, who is broader than our waywardness, and whose love is a greater force than our hate and disobedience. There is nothing in the heart of man that is outside the possibilities of God. We believe in one God infinitely perfect.

Atheism is not really our problem. Our problem is agnosticism. Many of can say—my God. I believe that no matter what your spiritual condition, most of you when the chips are down would say—yes, there is a God, there has to be a God. But how many of you can say with the Psalmist—I will say to the Lord, my refuge, my fortress, My God." How many of you know God personally so you can say—He is mine. You will notice in the end of the Scripture that we read, Psalm 91, what it is to have a relationship with God such as the Psalmist had. "Because he cleaves to me in love, I will deliver him." Who is saying that but God Himself? God is saying—because he cleaves to me and loves me I will deliver him. The person who has a personal relationship with God knows Him in His providence. He cares for him. God is working on behalf of His children. "When he calls to me I will answer and will be with him in trouble." The person who knows God personally knows God as a presence in times of affliction. I would be surprised to find a person who has not prayed, but I would not be surprised that some of you have prayed in the darkness of affliction and have gone away unanswered. Is that not true? Isn't it true that many of you know little of the presence of God, and your prayer is a prayer of desperation. You say—oh God, where are you—and then when the echo of your prayer finally reverberates into silence, you pick up and go on. How many of you know the presence of God sitting beside you when you weep? How many of you know the God who comes to you in the darkness of the night and you say—Oh God, my God, come to me. Quiet my heart, subdue this awful strain. How many of you know anything of that?

"I will rescue him and honor him. With long life I will satisfy him and show him my salvation." How many of you know the salvation of God—know the God who saves you, not only from your present sin but saves you eternally, saves you so that death has no terror for you, so that the grave does not stare you in the face, but that you are greater than all these things because God Himself has given you eternal life. In John 17 Jesus told us of this God and of this eternal life in His priestly prayer. He said, "And this is eternal life that they know Thee, the only true God, and Jesus Christ whom thou hast sent."

Atheism is not our problem. Our problem is that there are many of you who cannot say—my God, my God—because you do not know Him through Jesus Christ. Jesus Christ came to give us eternal life. He came to say that God loves you, He came to say that when you are in trouble God will come to you. He came to say that when you have sinned God will come and forgive that sin and heal your heart. He came to say that when you live in this world, God will live with you and be a presence with you, and He will lead you and guide you. This is my God.

ARTICLE III

We believe that Jesus Christ is true God and true man, having been conceived of the Holy Ghost and born of the Virgin Mary. He died on the cross a sacrifice for our sins according to the Scriptures. Further, He arose bodily from the dead, ascended into heaven, where at the right hand of the Majesty on High He now is our High Priest and Advocate.

CHAPTER THREE

THE CHRIST WE SERVE

The importance of Jesus Christ is an historical fact. No other figure on the plane of world history has had such profound and significant effect on the destiny and history of mankind. You will find more space devoted to Jesus Christ in the encyclopedias of the world than to any other historical personage. You will find that the entire world today deals in reference to time with the event of his birth, and every document that seeks to relate itself to some historical period must of necessity invoke the reality of Jesus Christ. How ever you attempt to explain the influence of Jesus Christ on the history of man, you cannot explain it away. Yet the question today is not why has this man had this influence, but it is the same one that Jesus Himself asked of His disciples in the eighth chapter of the Gospel of Mark, "Who do men say that I am?"

We begin with the assumption that He is the most important personage in the world and has been since His birth and will be as long as the history of man continues, so we are not attempting to prove His importance, but to answer the question He Himself asked, "Who do men say that I am?" Now it's a strange thing that a person of such historical importance should be unidentified. How strange that though we identify our age by reference to His birth, we have a myriad of opinions as to who He was, and we have on almost every corner of our cities some form of testimony as to who men think He was.

Let us begin with His name. You will find that in our Statement of Faith we have identified this person as Jesus Christ. Even our children in the nursery are taught of Jesus Christ, and the name of Jesus is one of the first names taught to a child in the Christian home. Your little children two years old can no doubt at least make a credible attempt to sing "Jesus Loves Me, This I Know." The name Jesus is not hard to pronounce, and it is not difficult to remember. Jesus Christ—now what does this mean? In Matthew chapter 1 the Scripture tells us that the angel said, "Thou shalt call His name Jesus because he shall save his people from their sins." So His very name speaks to us of His mission in life. "He shall save his people from their sins"—and so Jesus simply means Savior—Savior from sin.

We associate the name Christ with Jesus, and perhaps we have done this too quickly, not understanding the significance of it, for He was not always named Christ. He was named Jesus from His birth, but the name Christ became His name as others saw in Him a fulfillment of the Old Testament prophecy. The name Christ is the Greek form of the Hebrew word "messiah" which simply means "anointed one" or "one whom God anoints," and the Old Testament is full of references to God's anointing of certain individuals for a specific service. In Daniel 9:25 the Old Testament speaks of one who will come who will be the anointed one, who will be the Messiah; and so in the time of Jesus the Jewish people had been looking for at least 400 years for this individual who would have a right to the name "Messiah". It is interesting that in the Gospel of John, chapter 1, when Andrew came to Simon after speaking with Jesus, verse 41, "He first found his brother Simon and said to him, we have found the Messiah." He didn't say—we have found Jesus Christ. He said—we have found the Messiah. Of course he spoke of Jesus of Nazareth, the carpenter; but very early in the ministry of Jesus there was this recognition that He was more than just a carpenter, He was more than just a good man; He stood in direct fulfillment of the Old Testament finger which was pointing to a certain individual yet unnamed who would be the Messiah.

Now what did Jesus Himself make of this? In the fourth chapter of John we have an explicit confirmation from Jesus Himself that this was true, that He was the Messiah of which the Old Testament speaks. In this section of Scripture, John 4, Jesus was speaking to the woman by the Samaritan well. In verse 24 Jesus has said, "God is spirit, and those who worship him must worship in spirit and truth," and the woman said, "I know that Messiah is coming" and then in parentheses "he who is called Christ." Here you have the Greek word which is the equivalent to the Hebrew word "messiah." "When he comes, he will show us all things." Jesus said to her, "I who speak to you am he." I am the Messiah. He confirmed this in other instances. In Acts 9:22 the Apostle Paul preached immediately after his conversion, and what was his message? "Saul increased all the more in strength, and confounded the Jews who lived in Damascus by proving that Jesus was the Christ." So that Jesus Christ is simply the way of representing the historical person Jesus with the divine representation, the Messiah, God's anointed one, who will come to save and to redeem.

Now let us speak of Jesus Christ. In our Statement of

Faith we have listed certain things that speak of His theological identity. We speak of such things as being conceived by the Holy Ghost, dying as a sacrifice for sins, rising from the dead, ascending to heaven, sitting at the right hand of God the Father. All of these things speak to us of the theological significance of His life. Let us break this down into a very simple outline of who Jesus was, and we will turn to the book of Colossians and find in the first three chapters a marvelous exposition of Jesus Christ in certain aspects of His person in relationship to God and His relationship to man. Col. 1:15-20 speaks of Jesus Christ. "He is the image of the invisible God, the first-born of all creation, for in him all things were created, in heaven and on earth, visible and invisible, whether thrones or dominions or principalities or authorities—all things were created through him and for him. He is before all things, and in him all things hold together. He is the head of the body, the church; he is the beginning, the first-born from the dead, that in everything he might be pre-eminent. For in him all the fulness of God was pleased to dwell, and through him to reconcile to himself all things, whether on earth or in heaven, making peace by the blood of his cross." Here we see Christ the image of God.

There are three words in the New Testament that speak of this same basic thought, three different words, and it is interesting to trace just briefly the significance of the word. In verse 15 we have the word translated "image". "He is the image of the invisible God." The Greek word is *eikon*. We have an English word that is equivalent. We speak of an icon, meaning a small representation of a divinity, a god, an image that is worshipped. An iconoclast is one who breaks images, and the person today who goes around destroying things that others hold dear will be called an iconoclast. He breaks images, he destroys all things that we cherish. So that *eikon* "image" is meant to be a representation, an outline of a shadowy reality in tangible form. Now God is a very shadowy reality when He is only a spirit; and when you deal in the realm of spiritual things, there is no profile except the profile emerged in historical form, so that you could substitute the word "profile" for "image". He is the profile of the invisible God. It is almost as if you had a photographic plate upon which the impression had been made, but when you look at it there is nothing there because it is invisible. When you immerse this in the proper fluid, suddenly the profile emerges—it has been there all the time but we cannot see it until it takes shape. He is the profile, the image, of the invisible God.

In Hebrews 1 there is another reference to this same idea, but using a different word. Hebrews 1:3 "He reflects the glory of God and bears the very stamp of his nature." The King James version reads "express image" but it's not the same word used in Col. 1:15. This is the Greek word *karacter* and you immediately recognize it because of the English word "character". He is the *karacter* of God. Now character is more than just a profile. Character is that which has been engraved, and the verb form of this word is actually the word you would use to engrave something, to make the impression upon something else of another reality. We use the word "character" to define something that we symbolize. Words are a series of characters drawn out and these characters symbolize a certain reality. So that Christ is the *karacter* of God—the character of God, the essence of who God is, and imprinted not just as a profile, but everything that God is has made its mark on humanity. Everything is filled in, every detail has left an impression. He is the imprint of God's glory in humanity.

One other place refers to the same thought and uses a different word, John 1:18. "No one has ever seen God," John says, "the only Son, who is in the bosom of the Father, he has made him known." This is very inadequate to express the Greek word. The other two words were fairly familiar *eikon* and *karacter*—because you could associate English words with them. If you are a student of God's Word in a technical sense someone might say that you are an "exegete". Exegesis is simply the critical study of God's Word so as to bring out of the Word all of the truth. An exegetical study of the Word is a study of the text in order to lead forth the truth so that it can be grasped with the mind and understood. Exegesis is an intense study, but the purpose of exegesis is to illuminate, to lead forth, through exposition. This is the word used here. Jesus Christ has "exegeted" God, He has led forth out of the profound depth of God's nature the truth of who God is in ways we can understand.

In Colossians 1:19 we have stated in terms that cannot be misunderstood "In him all the fulness of God was pleased to dwell." I will not labor the mystery of how Jesus could be both God and man. I will only repeat that He was fully God and completely man, and there is no other way to state it than to say that He was both God and man. He was not a synthesis of God in man so that He became partly God and partly man. He was as human as each of us, and He was as much divine as God the Father. Jesus said of Himself—He that has seen Me has seen the Father, I and the Father are one. Jesus forgave sin, and the Pharisees said—who can forgive sin but God only—and Jesus said—that's just the point, I have forgiven your sin, and which is easier to believe that I can say your sins are forgiven or pick up your bed and walk, but that you might know that the Son of Man has authority on earth to forgive sins, pick up your bed and walk. Christ the image of God, and we are speaking now not so much of who Jesus was but who God is. God is Jesus.

In chapter 2 of Colossians we move from Christ, the image of God, to Christ the wisdom of God. Paul says, "I want you to know how greatly I strive for you, and for those at Laodicea, and for all who have not seen my face, that their hearts may be encouraged as they are knit together in love, to have all the riches of assured understanding and the knowledge of God's mystery, of Christ, in whom are hid all the treasures of wisdom and knowledge." I like to speak to college students and read this verse to them and say, "Do you realize that in Jesus Christ all of the wisdom of God is revealed. Now think of the long hours you've spent cramming for an exam—think of the hours of tedious discipline you've gone through in order to learn something, and here Jesus Christ is the wisdom of God. Don't you think that through Jesus Christ you wouldn't have to study?" Now momentarily they like this idea, but invariably a few hands are raised and they say, "But this is not what it means." All right, what does it mean? If Jesus Christ is the wisdom of God, what does it mean?

Quickly turn back to I Cor. 1 and we shall trace through the thought of how Jesus Christ is God's wisdom. Paul is speaking of wisdom and foolishness. Let us begin with verse 20, "Where is the wise man? Where is the scribe? Where is the debater of this age? Has not God made foolish the wisdom of the world? For since in the wisdom of God the world did not know God through wisdom, it pleased God through the folly of what we preach to save those who believe." Apparently God's wisdom is not the technical scientific wisdom of the world because Paul has said that in spite of all men's knowledge he ends up a fool and cannot save himself, so in the face of all man's wisdom God comes with a wisdom that appears to be foolish. It's the message that we preach, that Jesus Christ died, that God died. Now that doesn't make much sense from the standpoint of logic and science but this is God's wisdom—God died for man. Paul says in verse 22, "For Jews demand signs and Greeks seek wisdom, but we preach Christ crucified . . ." So that God's wisdom is involved with God's dying for man.

We can trace the same thought through in Ephesians. In the first chapter Paul speaks of the mystery of Christ. In the third chapter he picks up the thought of mystery and relates it to the wisdom of God through Jesus Christ. Verse 10, "That through the church the manifold wisdom of God might now be made known to the principalities and powers in the heavenly places."

Suppose that on a local high school campus, a boy who has moved from the San Francisco area with his parents appears bright and early on a Monday morning. Now he would be a stranger; there would be very little knowledge about him, and of course the girls on campus would want more information and would begin asking questions—who is he—and someone would say—his name is Joe Brown. We now have some knowledge about him, he's no longer quite so much a stranger, and in talking with Joe some more knowledge comes out: he's 16 years of age and he's got his driver's license. Fine, more knowledge, interesting knowledge. And through a period of a week or so a lot of information is disseminated throughout the campus about Joe Brown. He is no longer a stranger.

One girl says—I still don't know too much about him, but I remember I have a cousin up in San Francisco who attended the same school. So she writes to her cousin and says—did you know Joe Brown? The girl writes back and says—did I know Joe Brown—oh, yes! So she writes a 3-page typewritten letter on both sides with information about Joe Brown, and the girl adds this to her file. Now suppose this particular girl thinks she has enough information about Joe Brown so she wants to get to know him better, so she secures a date, and on that date they talk and she discovers more information about Joe. Joe doesn't like onions on his hamburgers, he likes Fords, not Chevrolets, he likes this and not that, he likes poetry and not novels. She's getting a lot of information about Joe, she finds she's attracted to him, and in little ways indicates to him how much she thinks of him. Yet week after week go by, date after date, and there's something missing. She has all the knowledge of Joe any person could ever ask, she knows what he thinks, she knows his problems, his joys. But there's one thing she doesn't know about Joe, and that is what he thinks of her, because he's never said—I love you—and only he can say it. And until Joe reveals himself, there is a lot of knowledge in the relationship but no wisdom, because the wisdom of the relationship is the revelation of who he is towards her.

Now if you quickly transfer this analogy into the realm of our relationship with God, we can search the heavens and the creation and the Bible, and we can gain a lot of knowledge about who God is, but until God speaks to us and says—I love you—there is no wisdom in the relationship. And Jesus Christ is the wisdom of God. It is God saying through Christ—I love you. "For God so loved the world that he gave his only Son, that whoever believes in him should not perish but have eternal life." Jesus Christ is the wisdom of God because He is the revelation of God's heart toward man—I love you, I am concerned about you, I know you by name. And suddenly our relationship with God moves from knowledge into wisdom, and there is a mutual relationship established.

Jesus Christ is the image of God, He is the wisdom of God, and He is also the Lord of life. Listen to what Paul says, "If then you have been raised with Christ, seek the things that are above, not on things that are on earth. For you have died, and your life is hid with Christ in God. When Christ who is our life appears, then you also will appear with him in glory." (Col. 3:14). You will note our Statement of Faith speaks to us not simply of a Christ who died but a Christ who is raised, a contemporary Christ, a Christ who now lives to be the Lord of life, who is the pulse beat of every heart. Christ not to be worshipped from afar, but Christ to be known within the heart. Not only did Christ come that God might say to us—I love you —but Christ came that God might reach into our hearts and redeem us from the sin that enslaves us. Paul has said in Col. 1:27, "Christ in you, the hope of glory." Christ at the right hand of God because He is the intercessor, Christ who has ascended into heaven because He is now sovereign over all of life, but Christ in the heart of man because Christ came to redeem and to ennoble and to cause the affections of the heart to rise to good things. "Set your minds on things above" because Christ is the Lord of life.

Oh, we believe in Jesus Christ—how easy it is to say that, but what a difference it makes when we say—Jesus Christ is in me and my life is different. Watch it—watch me when I walk out of here, watch me at my work, watch me when the pressure is on and when tension grips my heart, watch me when I'm tempted to be at my worst, and you will see that Jesus Christ lives in me. Jesus said—who am I to you—who do you think I am? Peter said—you are Messiah, you are my Lord, you are my Christ. Until you have said it, He is not yours. "If then you have been raised with Christ, seek the things that are above. . . . When Christ who is our life appears, then you also will appear with him in glory" (Col. 3:1,4). Aren't you glad that you believe in Jesus Christ, and that God has said—I love you?

ARTICLE IV

We believe that the ministry of the Holy Spirit is to glorify the Lord Jesus Christ, and during this age to convict men, regenerate the believing sinner, indwell, guide, instruct, and empower the believer for godly living and service.

CHAPTER FOUR

THE SPIRIT WE KNOW

Perhaps the Spirit of our age can best be summed up as the age of the optional accessory. Most everything we buy for our homes and our cars deals with accessories. This is a strange age because of this, and perhaps some of this has crept into our experience and even into our theology. We have been betrayed by this same spirit so that one's experience of God has a basic definition and beyond that are many optional accessories, and it depends upon how serious you want to be.

You can have a relationship with God which at most is functional and convenient, and then if you want to become more serious and more "religious" you can add a few accessories such as a devotional life, some consistent form of study of God's

Word, perhaps a few functions within the church itself, and if you really want to go all the way, you can dabble in the things of the Holy Spirit. I choose these words carefully because this is what I believe is so shocking about our age, that the ministry of the Holy Spirit is considered an optional accessory for those who wish to dabble in spiritual things. Ah, this is a tragic thing because when the Holy Spirit becomes a personal status symbol or a means of personal gratification, then we have lost the very person of God Himself, and we have distorted the Christian relationship to God through Jesus Christ. In the Word of God we shall discover a clear and unambiguous teaching concerning the person and ministry of the Holy Spirit and His relevance for us, the necessity of the Holy Spirit in the believer's life.

Let us speak first of all of the person of the Holy Spirit. It would seem needless to say that He is not a thing but a person, and yet one of the things that most of us have to soon learn is not to refer to the Holy Spirit as "it". Suppose someone thought of you as "it". Suppose a boy or girl were going out together and the boy would say—well, I have to take "it" out tonight—how would you like that? Suppose husbands and wives spoke of each other as "it"—wouldn't that be a degrading thing in a relationship—an impossible thing? At the outset let us remember that when we speak of the Holy Spirit we are speaking of a person and a personality, a living being, God Himself. We are not speaking of something that can be placed on a shelf or dissected with the tools of theology to discover what it is. We are speaking of a person, and when you speak of a person, all the dignity of a personal relationship has to be there from the beginning. There must be humility, there must be commitment, there must be honesty, there must be searching. Do not deceive your hearts—he who comes to God must believe that He is, and when we speak of the things of God, we must come to God as a person and share in His life, in His relationship.

Yet the Holy Spirit as the third person of the Trinity is perhaps the most mystifying. God the Father we can understand because we know of fathers, Jesus the Son we can understand because we know of sons, and He was of such sonship that He could be touched, He spoke words that we can understand, and He died a death that is common to all of us. But what shall we say of the Holy Spirit? How shall we identify, how shall we discern the profile of the Holy Spirit? There is reason for the mystery of the Holy Spirit, and it is because the Holy Spirit as the third person of God is revealed in the most intimate relationship in order that man might come into intimate relationship with God.

The question very often asked is—does the Old Testament speak of the Holy Spirit? As a matter of fact, yes, but very subtly. In the Old Testament we find many references to the spirit of God and God's spirit, but there are only two places in which the phrase "the Holy Spirit of God" is used. When the Greek translation of the Old Testament was made, in these two places the same phrase used in the New Testament some 80 or 90 times and translated "the Holy Spirit" was used in the Old Testament. This gives us a faithful guide as to the meaning of the phrase. The first reference is found in Psalm 51:11. In this familiar Psalm David, broken by his sin, speaks to God in terms of forgiveness, and his prayer includes a very specific prayer concerning the Holy Spirit. "Create in me a clean heart, O God, and put a new and right spirit within me. Cast me not away from thy presence, and take not thy Holy Spirit from me." Isa. 63:10 is the other reference in the Old Testament to the Holy Spirit.

The word "spirit" as used in the Old Testament and in the New has a very distinctive origin. It is the word for "wind" or "breath." In the first chapter of Genesis the Scripture speaks of God in relationship to His creation, and in the first and second verses we have a reference to God's Spirit. "In the beginning God created the heavens and the earth, and the earth was without form and void, and darkness was upon the face of the deep; and the Spirit of God was moving over the face of the waters." Now this literally reads, "The breath of God was brooding over the waters." In Gen. 2:7 speaking of the creation of man, "Then the Lord God formed man of the dust of the ground and breathed into his nostrils the breath of life and man became a living being." And the word for "breath" is the word "spirit"—the same word used in "the Holy Spirit." It is significant that God breathed into man, and man has breath, and that this breath is spirit. There is a wonderful symbolism when we move from the thought of a man's breath, the breath of life, and the spirit of life; so throughout the Scriptures both Old and New Testaments the word for "spirit" is the word "breath" or "wind." But very quickly this wind and breath is associated with life itself so that man who has the breath of life has the spirit of life, and the source of man's breath and spirit is the breath of God.

Along this line it is interesting to think of the significance of the relationship between the breath and the word of one speaking, that the word that is spoken is propelled by the breath of a man, and if we think of the Son of God, Jesus Christ, as the Word of God, the Spirit of God is the breath of God which breathes the Word, that the breath of God is the energizing, moving Spirit of God, so that when the Word is there in its profile, the breath has been responsible and is distinctly related to it. Ought this not to teach us that a man's breath has no profile but his words do; nonetheless, the breath is real and the spirit is real. So that when we speak of the Holy Spirit we are not seeking to find a profile, but we are seeking to find the energy, we are seeking to find the spirit behind that which is spoken. In John 20:22 after the resurrection, you remember these words, "Jesus breathed on his disciples and said, Receive the Holy Spirit." This is why we sing the hymn "Breathe on us, Breath of God." We are asking that God's Spirit should move upon us and within us so that God's life shall become our life.

Let us trace through the Old Testament some references to the Holy Spirit, to the Spirit of God in his progression through redemptive experience. First, from Exodus 31, "The Lord said to Moses, 'See I have called by name Bezalel the son of Uri, son of Hur, of the tribe of Judah; and I have filled him with the Spirit of God (or the breath of God), with ability and intelligence, with knowledge and all craftsmanship, to devise artistic designs, to work in gold, silver, and bronze, in cutting stones for setting, and in carving wood, for work in every craft.' " Isn't it interesting that the Spirit of God enhances and perfects the natural attributes of man so that such things as ability and intelligence and knowledge and craftsmanship are intensified when moved by the Spirit of God. There is a sense in which the Spirit of God can perfect and enhance man's natural abilities. Then from II Sam. 23:2. These are the words of David, "The Spirit of the Lord speaks by me, his word is upon my tongue." If we read this literally it reads—the breath of God speaks by me, his words are upon my tongue" so that human words have a divine breath; and of course we are led here to the very real truth of inspiration—God-breathed Scripture. We find this in the New Testament, II Tim. 3:16, "All Scripture is inspired by God"—God breathed. David said—God's breath produces the words on my tongue—so that we find in the Old Testament a very real concept of God's Spirit interpreting His will through human words, and here we have the words of prophecy.

As a corollary reference to this thought you will find II Peter 1:21 says, "Men moved by the Holy Spirit spoke from God." In Isaiah 11 is another reference to the Spirit of God in relationship to men and to man. Here we find a prophecy concerning the Messiah who will come, beginning with verse 1, "There shall come forth a shoot from the stump of Jesse, and a branch shall grow out of his roots, and the Spirit of the Lord shall rest upon him, the spirit of wisdom and understanding, the spirit of counsel and might, the spirit of knowledge and the fear of the Lord." Here we have the concept of God's Spirit anointing a man for special service, and through the word "anointing" we have the word "Messiah". Jesus Himself recognized this, and in Matthew 3:16 we have the account of the Holy Spirit descending upon Jesus at his baptism, and in Luke 4:18 Jesus speaking in the synagogue, "The Spirit of the Lord is upon me, because he has anointed me to preach good news to the poor"—the breath of God breathed on him, the anointing of God, the preparation and the credentials for a divine ministry of redemption.

Once more in Psalm 51 we find perhaps the high point of the ministry of God's Spirit in the Old Testament, and this is the ministry of inward cleansing and perfection. Verse 10, "Create in me a clean heart, O God, and put a new and right spirit within me. Cast me not away from thy presence, and take not thy Holy Spirit from me"—so that God's breath, His presence, His Spirit produced in man an inward righteousness, a purging from sin, a cleansing from sin.

Yet there is something more to be said concerning the Holy Spirit, and this of course is the relationship of the Holy Spirit to the church; and we must turn immediately to chapter 2 of the Book of Acts, because having understood the development of God's Spirit in the Old Testament in relation to redemption, we must see the Day of Pentecost as a fulfillment of all that the Old Testament intimated concerning God's Spirit. "When the day of Pentecost had come, they were all together in one place. And suddenly a sound came from heaven like the rush of a mighty wind (and remember that the Spirit is the breath of God) and it filled all the house where they were sitting. And there appeared to them tongues as of fire, distributed and resting on each one of them. And they were all filled with the Holy Spirit and began to speak in other tongues, as the Spirit gave them utterance" (Acts 2:1-4).

The person of the Holy Spirit is the presence of God breathed into human experience in such a way that there is an inspiration for human life, a perfecting of human capabilities, a cleansing of the human heart but a filling and empowering for witnessing and speaking, because now the ministry of the Holy Spirit must be to complete the ministry of the Word of God through us. So that we now speak the words that are the words of God, and Jesus Christ who is the Word of God literally speaks through us and continues His ministry of witnessing to His own death and resurrection. Why is it important that the Holy Spirit dwells in the heart of the believer? Because unless the Holy Spirit dwells in the heart, God's Word is silent and

Jesus Christ has no existence in this world. Because Christ is at the right hand of the Father, He can dwell on the earth only as the Spirit of God dwells in man.

The Holy Spirit's ministry is to glorify Jesus Christ, and let us now turn from the person of the Holy Spirit to the ministry of the Holy Spirit. First of all, we shall have to clarify the ministry of the Holy Spirit as to His relationship with Christ, and secondly, as to His relationship with man. Note John 16:7, "Nevertheless I tell you the truth; it is to your advantage that I go away, for if I do not go away, the Counselor will not come to you; but if I go, I will send him to you." Now this is an important thought and a helpful one to remember that the Holy Spirit has a distinct relationship to Jesus Christ, so that what Jesus was saying was that as long as I am here on earth with you, the Holy Spirit cannot come—because there is no confusion in the trinity.

If our minds are confused, God is not confused about His own nature. God the Father is the Creator of the universe and the Father of us all; Jesus Christ is the eternally begotten son of the Father, having existed eternally with the Father but always as the expression of the Father's love; and the Holy Spirit has existed eternally along with the Father and the Son as the effectual presence of God's love as expressed through God's Son. So the right order of redemption is a clue to the meaning of the Holy Spirit in His appearance, that first of all, the Father has created, then the expression of love came to us and spoke of redemption, and now He must return to the right hand of the Father in order that the Spirit of God might come to dwell within man because Jesus Christ cannot dwell bodily in every person. But when the Spirit of God abides in man, God the Father abides in him, because God is love; Christ the Son abides in him, because the Son is love and is God; and so we rightly say that the Holy Spirit is the fullness of God dwelling in the human heart, and yet God the Father and Jesus the Son are not confused with the person of the Holy Spirit. Jesus said—it is to your advantage that I go to heaven in order that the Holy Spirit (God) may dwell in hearts and the presence of

God be experienced in human existence.

In John 16:14 we have a further thought concerning the relationship of the Holy Spirit to Jesus Christ. "He will glorify me," said Jesus, "for he will take what is mine and declare it to you." Then Jesus said, "All that the Father has is mine—therefore, when he takes what is mine and declares it to you, he is taking everything that is the Father's also." The ministry of the Holy Spirit is to find Himself in the reality of the Son and the Father, and this is the reason why the Holy Spirit has no profile of His own—the profile of the Holy Spirit is the indwelt heart of a believer. There is no presence of the Holy Spirit in this world apart from indwelt human personality. The Holy Spirit has only one home, and that is a human soul; and when we speak of the Holy Spirit apart from the human personality, we distort His nature. When the human personality is indwelt of God, the profile of that life becomes the profile of the Holy Spirit—and what is that profile? That we might be conformed to the image of His Son. Only the Son of God has a profile of God because He is the Word of God. Can we linger with that to grasp it—that the Father who is the Father of love has only one profile and that is the Word that expresses love in relationship to creation and to redemption. The ministry of the Holy Spirit is then to take Jesus Christ who is the Word of God and perfect Him in human experience.

How is this done? Through three things, and we have these in John, Chapter 16. First, Jesus said—when the Holy Spirit comes, He will convict or convince the world of sin. The Holy Spirit is what brings about in your heart that first twinge that you are wrong, oh, terribly wrong. He brings about in your heart that first intimation of guilt, when your heart despairs and becomes heavy and when you sense there is something wrong. In spite of your brazen attempts to live out your life, down deep in your heart there is something that will not sink beneath the waves of your unconscious mind, there is that lingering memory that you are wrong and have failed and no amount of excusing or rationalizing will take care of it. It is the Holy Spirit who is a faithful witness to the sin of your life, and He does this through the Word of God, He does this through the word of a friend, He does this through the conscience that witnesses to your own heart there's something wrong—don't do it, come and make it right. The Holy Spirit convinces the world of sin.

The Holy Spirit regenerates, makes new. David said—O God, create in me a new clean heart. Don't just paint the old one over, God, please don't just tie the dirty ends together and make a new bundle—O God, come in and so possess me that you have purged me of the torn and the spotted. Come in, God, and renew that which you once gave to me. Take away that sinking feeling, take away that predisposition to fail, give me a new and right spirit. Listen, when God meets man, something new takes place in his heart, and this is the ministry of the Holy Spirit that when the Word of God is preached the Spirit of God enters into the heart of man and something comes alive. We ought to understand that until God has come alive in our life all of our faith is pretense and professionalism. We have no right to say that we know God until the Spirit of God has entered into our life and there is a change, something new within.

Do not be fooled by thinking that faith is a religion you were born with. I read the obituary of a man I knew very well and there was a desperate attempt to satisfy the insecurity of the human heart by saying—"he was baptized into such and such a faith." What does that mean—will you tell me? I was baptized into a faith, but there came a moment when God Himself had to convict my heart of my sin, and I had to say—all right, God, you are right and I am wrong, now God, do something with this heart, come in and take over my life. It wasn't the words that I said—it was the fact that God is real. The ministry of the Holy Spirit is that no matter how confused and broken our words are, God enters into a heart that is repentant and honest —and God took up residence in my heart. Don't ever say of me—he was baptized into some faith—say of me, that in a dark night the living God entered into my heart in a mysterious transaction in which a seed of faith took root and could not be cast out even by my own failure, because where God dwells the Holy Spirit begins to transform and grow into a reality that is sufficient in itself, because the Holy Spirit is the fullness of God.

The person of the Holy Spirit, the ministry of the Holy Spirit, and then the gift of the Holy Spirit. On the day of Pentecost men whose hearts were stricken said to Peter—what then shall we do—and Peter didn't say—pray for the Holy Spirit. He said—repent and the gift of the Holy Spirit will be given to you. It took me many years to come to the place where I knew what was the necessary thing to do and it wasn't to pray for the Holy Spirit. The thing to do was to become honest with God and say—God, here I am for what I am. Here I am, exposed, enter into my life, forgive my sin. And behold, I received the gift of the Holy Spirit—a faith that cannot be lost; a memory of God's presence that cannot be effaced; a drive towards that which is better than I'd ever known; a constant conviction that just to try is not enough; a constant knowledge that nothing less than fellowship with God is sufficient for my heart.

Ah, yes, we believe in the Holy Spirit because our hearts believe that unless God moves and touches us we are lost and undone; we believe that the Holy Spirit can change us, can make our life a different one. What must we do? Repent— dare we discuss the Holy Spirit and not know that we have talked with God face to face. And what will you do, having talked with God face to face? Take a few notes and then say— oh, yes, now I understand something about the ministry of the Holy Spirit—and ignore the person of God? Oh, no—in the person of God there is the look of God, there is that moment in which you are in fellowship with God. If I could give you the gift of the Holy Spirit and put in your heart what God has put in mine, I would walk up to you and one by one I would lay my hands on your heads, and give you the gift of the Holy Spirit. God followed me through many years of pretense, of loneliness, He followed me into the midst of a dark night, and there in that darkness there was nothing left to say except— all right, God, I repent. And this is *your* action. What must you *do?* Repent—and God will dwell in your heart.

ARTICLE V

We believe that man was created in the image of God but fell into sin and is therefore lost and only through regeneration by the Holy Spirit can salvation and spiritual life be obtained.

CHAPTER FIVE

THE HUMAN PREDICAMENT

It is not strange that a Statement of Faith which seeks to encompass the entire horizon of the doctrine of God should include a statement concerning the identity of man. This is not strange because it is almost impossible to define God without understanding man, for we are men. You will notice in this statement concerning man that there is nothing of man's biological or physiological definition. The Bible is not redundant; that is, it does not repeat what can be discovered through human knowledge. The Bible has a clear and specific purpose, and that is to reveal God as a God of creation and redemption; and through that revelation to include all of the history and science necessary to give redemption an objective framework.

This means that anthropology is a true science and a meaningful curriculum for any Christian. We ought to understand what anthropology can teach us concerning who man is and what his history has been on earth, for much of this you will not find in the Bible. Strangely enough, man today thinks that through the study of anthropology and the science of physiology and bio-chemistry he has a sufficient understanding of himself so that he can dare to make pronouncements concerning the meaning of his life. It is one thing to have some understanding of the science of life; it is another to have an understanding of the meaning of life.

Our Statement of Faith contains certain indispensable truths concerning the identity of man and his nature. We shall select three phrases so that you may have a frame of reference for our thinking, and you may have something to take with you that is meaningful concerning who man is and meaningful concerning your own life. The first phrase obviously is that man was created. This speaks to us of the origin of man, and we must understand something of the origin of man—not that we are simply curious about the history of our ancestors, but we are rightly curious as to the reason for our own existence. The problem of the origin of man is not simply the problem of the origin of Adam, the first man, but the origin of our own spirit and gift of life.

The Bible speaks in two ways concerning the creation of man: first, his relationship to his creator, and then his relationship to all of creation. Let us begin in Genesis, Chapter 2. Some of these familiar Scriptures are very important to us in understanding the origin of man and his nature. We have said that man is created—now what does this mean?

You take several pieces of lumber from the lumber yard, and if you have a sharp saw and a hammer and a nail or two and not too many thumbs and an idea, you can change those random pieces of lumber into a meaningful and useful utensil. You can make a chair if you have the idea of a chair. No one has ever made a chair by accident—except someone like me who tried to make a table that was too low. But who would know enough to call it a chair unless you had the idea of a chair—it would be just a poor table. You'd have to sit on it, there'd be nothing else to do. Is this creation? Have I created something by taking random pieces of lumber that already were in existence and fashioning them into that which I had in my mind and can now use?

You take a piece of blank canvas and a few assorted colors. By applying the colors a certain way you can bring to life on that canvas an image that symbolizes a reality that you recognize, a reality of beauty, a reality of design, a reality of feeling, a reality of landscape. Now is that creation? There has to be the idea, and yet we do recognize that something has taken place that was not there before. Is this creation?

We have said that man is created—what does that mean? Does that mean a few pieces of lumber have fallen into place and someone says—oh, that looks like a chair—not having had the idea of a chair before? Does this mean that some bit of protoplasm in some mythical sea suddenly fell into some pattern that was functional and fruitful so that it finally could say of itself—oh, there is a man. Without the idea of a man? What *is* creation?

Can we say this, that first of all creation has to be an idea. When we say that God created man, we are saying that man was an idea before he became a reality and that the Bible wants us to understand that man was not an accident. But if you work your way back through the anthropology of the curriculum and are forced to define man by that which you can see of him, you can only say that apparently he *was* an accident, a genetic accident, and that the first bit of life was only a freak in which something came into existence without design or purpose. For who would dare to say that there was an idea before there was existence? No scientist, if he is a good scientist. A scientist is forced to explain what he sees. He dare not go beyond what he sees and say—there is an idea. This is why at the outset we make no apology for appealing to God's Word for some indication of who man is, because God's Word purports itself to be the idea that existed before existence, that God who had the design in his heart for fellowship with some other creature created man. And we know this because God told us, and if He hadn't told us we would never know it. Now the question to answer is not simply how did God create man, but can we understand God's definition of man?

Genesis 2:7 reads, "Then the Lord God formed man of dust from the ground, and breathed into his nostrils the breath of life; and man became a living being." Now here there is a separate creative act from that of animals. There is a sense of immediate creation, not so much from the standpoint of how long it took, but how it came about, and we are to understand that man is not an accident which has come about through some previous existence but man whoever he is has come about directly through a creative act of God. In making this statement, we are in no way infringing ourselves on the rightful science of anthropology which tells us how man lived in his first existence and what he was like. This is why we use the word that man was immediately created, instead of instantly created by God, because when we use the word "instantly" we are speaking of time, and we do not know whether it took one second or five minutes. We should beware of using words that do not allow us the freedom to discover truth in other areas. The minute we have chosen a doctrinal position that excludes a rightful field of human science we have put Christianity in a precarious position.

There are still Christians today who try to force upon the human mind the idea that man is about 600 years old and that this is all the information a person needs to understand the history of man. Scientists tell us that man has been on the face of the earth for at least 10,000 years and probably much longer. According to their findings these people are forced to set that aside as being untrue because they have already committed themselves to a concept that leaves no room for human science. Now this is foolish and it does not honor God to misunderstand His Word. The Scripture teaches us that man was immediately created by God; that is, it came about through God's direct act. It doesn't tell us whether it took five seconds or five days. We do not know. We do know that man is a derived being of a Divine Creator.

The Scripture says that God breathed something of Himself into human existence, and the first man became a living soul because he became an extension of the divine soul. So that man is a derived being, and this is crucial to man, because if he is not constantly in a state of dependence he is not whole. This is why redemptive revelation is so important as a supplement of anthropology and to psychology because it teaches us it is a fallacy that human existence is complete in and of itself and explains for us why man is pursued with such a sense of estrangement. It is because he is created dependent, created in relationship, and he can only be defined in terms of relating himself. A person who is not in relationship is not a person, he is only a fragment, and you can take that fragment and lay him on a couch and expose all of his inner feelings and turmoil and drives, and you can try to explain his behavior by his compulsions, but you are dealing only with a fragment—oh, a fragment that eats and drinks and breathes and reproduces, but a fragment, because there is no relationship. A creator is important to the existence of the human personality and not just as an idea to account for the origin of man. We need a creator as much as Adam did, because without a creator we are only a fragment. Without a creator Adam is only an accident. God breathed into the human body a divine spirit.

Those who would seek to explain the origin of man through the processes of evolution are doing the best they can with their own field, and we ought not to be shocked by the fact that they are trying to explain what they see. But on the other hand, they ought not to be so presumptuous as to think that what they see is everything. All we plead for is a recognition of the fields of truth. We are willing to accept truth wherever it is found, and we only ask that of the scientists. Truth itself is one, whether it is the truth that speaks to the heart or the truth that gives assurance to the mind or the truth of a mathematical formula. You see, man can be almost explained by evolution—almost. It almost makes sense, except that it still leaves man a fragment, and no person who is irrevocably committed to the theory of evolution is completely satisfied to simply be that. He wants more than that, and though he is forced intellectually to say—this is all I am—his heart says—but it isn't fair. And we believe that the truth of the heart demands an answer, and we believe that man needs a creator in order that his heart may have assurance that there is meaning to life.

Psalm 8 gives some reference to the relationship of man to creation, "Thou hast given him dominion over the works of thy hands." By the way, if anyone should ask you—do you think that man has the right to probe among the planets?—of course he does, for in Psalm 8 it speaks of the work of God's fingers as being the moon and stars, and in the same Psalm it says that God has given man dominion over the work of his fingers. Whatever God has touched is within the realm of man's dominion. And he is to explore, he is to subdue, he is to rule it. Why should we think our planet is the only thing that God created? Whatever God has created has been put within man's domain.

The second phrase in our Statement of Faith follows so closely to the first we would almost link them together, but they should be separated. First, we have said that man was created; the second phrase says, "in the image of God". The first phrase gives us a clue to the origin of man, and the second phrase of the nature of man. Man created in the image of God has certain characteristics that explain who he is and what his responsibilities are. Now this is very important because it tells us then that the true nature of man cannot be explained by anthropology by chemistry, by physiology, by psychology, because these are only descriptive sciences. You cannot look at the bones of a man who lived 10,000 years ago, you cannot even look at the environment in which he lived as you probe the ruins, and discover the image of God. For the knowledge that man was created in the image of God is a truth of special revelation—not of science. Of course there are evidences of this, once we know it. We see that wherever man has been found he has been a worshipping creature even if he has worshipped himself or idols. Wherever they find the ruins of man, they find some attempt on the part of that culture to express itself in worship. These are evidences that the image of God is at work, but they do not describe the image of God.

What is the image of God? Basically it is two things: it is moral agency, and moral excellency. This isn't so difficult because there is one word in both phrases that is the same, and the other two words aren't very difficult. Moral agency simply means that man has a moral capacity for knowledge of moral right and wrong; and moral excellency means he is moral himself. So that the original creation of God, Adam, had both moral agency (he knew right and wrong) and moral excellency (he was good). Now through sin Adam lost moral excellency, and he lost fellowship with God, but he still retained moral agency so that he was responsible to God.

Now then, we are in the human predicament, and the human predicament is that man is strangely enough still responsible to do good, but he is not good nor can he do good. And you say, this is unfair. No, it isn't. We deal the same way in our society. Suppose a person has, because of his environment and culture, been so conditioned that he has lost the capacity to prevent himself from committing a criminal act. Let us say he has become an inveterate thief and he cannot help himself. He lives on Skid Row and steals to make a living, and this is all he is, and because of his environment and his past he cannot help himself. Now let me ask you, is he still responsible for stealing when he steals? Yes, he is. Why? Because he knows that he ought not to steal though he cannot keep from stealing. And if you want to know whether or not he knows it's wrong to steal, you take from him what he has stolen and he'll say—you have no right to do that.

Take an individual who, because of an inadequately developed moral sense of right and wrong, though he is in an adult body, has no moral insight, and if that person commits a crime, is he guilty? No, and no judge in the land will convict a moral imbecile of a crime. So the ground of human responsibility is his knowledge of what is right and wrong, not his ability to do it. The image of God still works in man today because man has a conscience of wrong, and he has a carrying capacity for guilt, and his attempts to mediate his guilt and to modify it in many different ways are only an affirmation on his part that he has been created in the image of God and he is responsible.

Now then, where has this led us in the human predicament? Perhaps the finest statement of the human predicament we have in the Bible is found in Romans 1, beginning with verse 18, "For the wrath of God is revealed from heaven against all ungodliness and wickedness of men who by their wickedness suppress the truth. For what can be known about God is plain to them, because God has shown it to them." Here we understand that because man bears the image of God he has a sufficient knowledge of God so that he is responsible for obeying, yet the predicament is that man cannot obey. And why is that? The third phrase of our Statement of Faith says simply, "He fell into sin and is therefore lost."

There is no intelligent understanding of man without this truth—that he is lost; and to be lost means first of all that he is estranged, and not just estranged from God but estranged from himself. Man is lost because he is lonely and out of fellowship and in contradiction. Estrangement is a distortion of the self, estrangement is a loss of continuity between the divine breath and the human mind. Estrangement is the bearing of the silent guilt of who man is. Man created in the image of God is now lost, and only through regeneration can man become man, because regeneration restores the estrangement into intimacy. Regeneration is a new breathing in of God's life through the Holy Spirit.

Many times we are accused as Christians of being distorted people. That's true if you would allow the dead to judge the living and say the same thing. If you'd go out to the cemetery and ask the dead—what do you think of these creatures who are walking—they'd say—that sounds strange to us for people to be walking and breathing because we don't. When you compare a living man to a dead one, you would say there's a strangeness about a living man, and when you compare who has been born again with one who is estranged, there is strangeness because God has breathed into him new life through the Holy Spirit. He has new moral sensibilities, he has new moral capacity, but more than that he has a relationship with God that has solved the estrangement. There is a deep peace in his heart that he is man because he is now related to God, and he knows that the definition of himself is his relationship with God. Who is man? Man is God's child. Who are you? *Who* are you—a fragment struggling to understand yourself, bitterly resenting your estrangement?

Someone told a parable once about a typographical error that resented being corrected because the only reason for its existence was that it was an error. Strangely enough, many of you are protesting that you don't want to be changed and you cling to your estrangement because it's the only thing you've known. Now is this all you are—an error seeking to prolong its existence? Then I have news for you, you are more than an error. You are an idea. And until the error of your estrangement is corrected, the idea of who you are and who you can be shall never come into reality. God this very day can put within your heart once more His own life, and you shall become man.

ARTICLE VI

We believe that the shed blood of Jesus Christ and His resurrection provide the only ground for justification and salvation for all who believe, and only such as receive Jesus Christ are born of the Holy Spirit and thus become children of God.

CHAPTER SIX

THE DIVINE ENABLEMENT

The Statement of Faith has a logical progression. You will note that it began with the Word of God and moved through the doctrine of God Himself, to Jesus Christ, to man; and now we move to the solution of the human predicament.

The human predicament is essentially this—man is responsible but incapable. Through moral knowledge man is accountable to God to do the right, but he is incapable of consistently doing the right. Furthermore he is incapable of righting the wrong he has already done, so that man piles up guilt as he opens up awareness, and the more man knows, the more guilty he becomes and the more impossible becomes his situation. The human predicament is a real thing, and if there have been generations which sought to evade it, we are now in a generation which seeks to amplify the human predicament and in that amplification to find some measure of justification for the existence of man.

We said that the parable of the typographical error is that once the error has been made and if you give it personality, it will resist any attempt to rub it out, for after all it is only in existence because it is in error. Now the human predicament has a substance to it, and if man is essentially a problem, at least he has an identity, and the strange thing of our age, especially in the literary world, is that we are seeing the contradiction of the human predicament portrayed with stark realism, and we might add pessimism, until we have today the cult of unhappiness. The cult of unhappiness is the hope of man. I have a quotation from this month's Reader's Digest which is an excerpt from the speech John Steinbeck made when he accepted his Nobel prize: "Humanity has been passing through a grey and desolate time of confusion. The writer is delegated to declare and celebrate man's proven capacity for greatness of heart and spirit, for gallantry in defeat, for courage, compassion and love. In the endless war against weakness and despair, these are the bright rally flags of hope and emulation. I hold that a writer who does not passionately believe in the perfectibility of man has no dedication or any membership in literature."

If you have read anything of John Steinbeck you know that his flame of hope is black light, and you will find that his attempts to lift the human heart to greatness of soul is only by creating first of all the foundation of despair, as if the more despair there is, the more the human heart will dare to have the presumption to continue living. In fact, he betrays his own creed when he speaks of the endless war against despair and failure. There isn't much hope in an endless war, and if our only faith and hope and possibility is that we shall be courageous enough to continue a futile thing, this isn't a very bright profile for humanity.

THE DIVINE ENABLEMENT

The human predicament is real, and every man who deals with reality knows it. We have included in the Statement of Faith not only the reality of the human predicament, but the reality of a solution to the predicament—divine enablement. We stand unashamedly before the world and say that man does not have to submit to despair and to endless conflict against futility, that there is something better for man than this, and that this was God's intention from the beginning. This is the marvelous thing about salvation—it is not a latecomer on the scene of humanity. When we speak of redemption, we are not speaking of something that God thought of after it was almost too late. We often think of redemption as being solely limited to the cross and Christ's death, but it was in God's heart from the beginning to redeem man.

Let us begin with Genesis 3:15. At the very outset of man's existence he encounters the predicament. Adam's sin in the garden was that he betrayed his own righteousness and was left with moral knowledge of what he had done but was incapable of righting the wrong. God came to Adam, sought him out in that garden of sin, and not only clothed him but gave him a promise, "I will put enmity between you and the woman, and between your seed and her seed; he shall bruise your head, and you shall bruise his heel." Here God is speaking to Satan in the guise of the serpent. He is saying that there will be hostility between Satan and the woman "and between your seed and her seed". Now the seed of the serpent is the lingering malignancy of Satan and his agents in the world. The seed of the woman is eventually to culminate in Jesus Christ, and this Paul recognized in the book of Galatians. But the seed of the woman is that through man will come eventually the salvation of man, for this is what God said. "He shall bruise your head" that is, the seed of woman shall bruise the head of the serpent, "and you shall bruise his heel". It is one thing to be wounded; it is another thing to be destroyed; and while Jesus Christ was wounded for our transgressions, He destroyed the power of Satan, so we see that Christ did eventually fulfill this.

In Exodus we find that this redemption which has been

initiated in Genesis 3:15 is now demonstrated through God's dealings with the people of Israel. The people of Israel are in bondage in Egypt, and their deliverance from Egypt will be an object lesson of God's redemption. Exodus 3:6, "And he said, 'I am the God of your father, the God of Abraham, the God of Isaac, and the God of Jacob.' And Moses hid his face, for he was afraid to look at God. Then the Lord said, 'I have seen the affliction of my people who are in Egypt, and have heard their cry because of their taskmasters; I know their sufferings, and I have come down to deliver them out of the hand of the Egyptians, and to bring them up out of that land to a good and broad land, a land flowing with milk and honey, to the place of the Canaanites . . .' " Here we see that God's redemption was demonstrated in an object lesson as he took his people Israel out of the sin and bondage of Egypt into the land of promise and blessing and prosperity of Canaan. In Leviticus 17:11 we find that redemption is symbolized in its agency and in its effectiveness. "For the life of the flesh is in the blood; and I have given it for you upon the altar to make atonement for your souls; for it is the blood that makes atonement, by reason of the life."

So the Old Testament builds from the beginning a framework of redemption *initiated* in the garden, *demonstrated* as God took His people Israel out of Egypt, *symbolized* in the shedding of animal blood upon the altar, and *realized* as Jesus Christ came, the seed of woman, to give His life a ransom. Christ speaks of Himself in this very language in Matthew 20:28. This is one of the most important verses in the Gospels relating to the atonement of Jesus Christ, because it is Jesus' own words as to the purpose of His life. "Even as the Son of man came not to be served but to serve, and to give his life as a ransom for many." Jesus was not deceived. He knew that His life was to be a sacrifice, a payment of a penalty, to redeem, to ransom, to bring out of sin and bondage and hopelessness those who believe in Him.

Our Statement of Faith reveals for us something of the nature of this salvation which is the answer to the human predicament and which only God's Word presents. There is no human philosophy, there is no scientific discovery, there is no literary trick that will redeem man from his own predicament. First of all, would you note in the Statement of Faith that it is through the blood of Jesus Christ and His resurrection that justification and salvation is promised; in other words, God does not arbitrarily say—now I am going to decide to forgive all your sins. Why couldn't God do that?

When one of our children does something that incurs our wrath, we lay down a penalty and say—now you're going to be confined to your room all evening—and this is about four in the afternoon. Now this is pretty rough unless you have built-in TV, and it's worse if you're a teenager and there's no telephone. This is unacceptable and at the outset unendurable, and we spoke rashly because we planned to have them baby-sit later while we went out, so we've hurt ourselves more than them. Anyway, after about two hours of this injustice, can't the father or mother go into the room and say—well, you've suffered enough and I forgive you and everything is all right, come out of the room. Can't the mother or father do that? Certainly. It's within the discretion of the parent who administered the discipline to say—the discipline has now been effective and I abrogate what I first said, you don't have to stay in there all evening.

Why can't God do that? We are willing to recognize that we have sinned and are out of fellowship with God. Now if God really has as much compassion as we do for our children, why doesn't He walk over to the edge of heaven and look down and see how sorry we are for this predicament and say—children, you've suffered enough, I forgive you, everything is all right. He can't do that—and you know why. The answer is given in the Scripture which we read, Romans chapter 3. The death of Jesus Christ was not primarily to justify man but to vindicate God. The primary purpose of the death of Jesus Christ was to establish the righteousnss of God. "God put Christ forward as an expiation by His blood to be received by faith." This was to show God's righteousness, and why would God be liable to the charge of unrighteousness? Because God had already established that the soul that sins shall die.

God had already said that once sin has lost fellowship with God, there is no way back. And yet God forgave sin in the Old Testament. When men took the blood of goats and poured it forth upon the altar, God said, "I forgive your sin." Now what right has God to forgive something in which there has been no atonement? He doesn't have the right because God would be liable to the charge of injustice. Even a judge in our court system today would soon be taken off the bench if he started dispensing freedom without regard to penalty. Suppose that a judge went to the prisons of our state and said, "I'm going to open the doors, I have now decided there shall be no punishment." He cannot *do* that—the very principle of justice itself requires that penalty be paid, and it doesn't make any difference what extent of grief there is involved or how much repentance. Penalty itself is required by the offense. We believe that—we operate under those principles, and God Himself does too.

It is important that we understand that the basis of our salvation is not faith, but rather what Christ has done. Faith doesn't make anything true if it's untrue. Just believing something doesn't make it so, as Senator Everett Dirksen reminded us this week in the paper of the story concerning Abraham Lincoln who rebuked his colleagues who thought that politically they could make things white that were black. He said—suppose I call a sheep's tail a foot, how many feet does a sheep have? And the opponents would say—well, five. He'd say— no, it doesn't make any difference what you call a sheep's tail, it's still a tail. You can't just believe that everything is all right between you and God if it's not. There has to be a reason for you to believe it, and the reason we believe we are saved and belong to God is because of what Jesus Christ has done, so that His death and resurrection is the basis for our salvation; and when God saw that, He could turn to us and say— I now can accept you because the price is paid. When we speak about atonement and think about justification and redemption, we are only saying that God, because He has looked upon Jesus Christ dying for our sins, can now turn and look upon us and forgive us.

Now if that seems simple, it is also terribly profound because Jesus Christ was God Himself, He was God's own Son. Who died upon the cross? God died. Whose blood was shed? God's blood was shed, because Jesus said of Himself, "If you have seen me, you have seen God. I and the Father are one." How strange that God Himself should do for man what man could not do. Ah, but this is just the significance of who Jesus Christ was.

Notice that in the death of Christ or in His life His primary purpose was not that He should live a life of example, but that He should be born into the human predicament. In Gal. 4:4-5 we see the existence of Jesus carefully presented in its true form. He was not sent to earth to show us what we have not been doing—we knew that. He did not come to make us feel bad because we have sinned—we have already felt the pangs of sin. He did not come to trace a straight course as an example that we would know how to walk—we know what a straight line is. We knew what righteousness was before Christ came, but we did not know what love was—completely. We did not dare believe that love would die until love died.

Galatians 4:4-5 declares that Christ was sent when the time had come. "But when the time had fully come, God sent forth his Son, born of woman, born under the law, to redeem those who were under the law, so that we might receive adoption as sons." Christ was born *into* the human predicament, and when He was born He became part of the sin of the human race. He took upon Himself the nature of humanity. The fact that He had no personal sin does not mean that He did not accept the human predicament. He was born into it. In Hebrews 2:14 we find that the purpose of Jesus was not simply to be born but to die. "Since therefore the children share in flesh and blood, he himself likewise partook of the same nature, that through death he might destroy him who has the power of death, that is, the devil." If Jesus Christ had not died, could He have saved us? The answer is—no. It wasn't until His death that He finally tasted the bitterness of the human predicament, and in spite of what Steinbeck says, humanity is not perfectible of itself. It is marching inevitably over the precipice into death, and no matter how bravely you go over the precipice, no matter how much courage there is in your heart that it is worthwhile, there is no changing the inevitable course of the human heart, and that is the grave.

Now what if Jesus had come to earth and had suffered everything that we have suffered except death? It wouldn't have helped. What good is it to have someone experience with you almost everything that you suffer? He took upon Himself flesh and blood in order that He might die, and in dying He carried with Him all the possibilities and future of humanity. Love died. We did not think it would dare to die. We were not sure what would happen when love died. But because love is true to itself and has within itself its own power, and love is God, and God is love, when love died, when Jesus Christ died, God died. But God canot die; and the grave and the devil and Satan have no power over ultimate love, and so the grave could not contain Him, and that's why the word "resurrection" is in our Statement of Faith. Love died, but love now lives and because He carried with Him all of humanity into the grave He carried out of the grave all of the possibilities of human life.

Now then, the redemption of Jesus Christ is the basis for our salvation. It is the personal responsibility of every man. It is interesting to note that in I John 2:2 the Bible says that Jesus died for the sins of the whole world. Does this mean, and this is a serious question—does this mean that every person in the world is redeemed if Jesus died for all of the sins of the world. There are some who would say—yes, Jesus now has saved all of humanity. But if this were true, there would be no hint in Scripture that any would be lost but that all ultimately would be saved. But this is not true, and in John 10:26-28 Jesus said—there are some who do not belong to my sheep. I don't know who they are if they are not some of humanity. In Matthew 7:21-23 Jesus said—not everyone shall enter heaven. Do you understand that? Not everyone shall enter heaven. And it is a possibility that not every one in this room will enter heaven.

Let's make it personal, shall we. It is possible that not

every young person here shall enter heaven, shall grow up and be a believer. And I would say that it is more than just a possibility that some day some of you in this room shall not be believers. I say this is more than just a possibility because it happens every day. The children of Christian parents grow up and do not become believers, and the Scripture says of them—they shall not enter the kingdom of heaven. Many young people have been brought up in Sunday School and have participated in the youth activities and have entered into life and have forgotten the whole thing and have walked alone without faith in Jesus Christ in spite of prayers of parents and what Sunday School teachers have taught them, in spite of how often they have heard the gospel.

Jesus died for the sins of the whole world, but only such as believe in Him are born of the Holy Spirit, and you can take that line in the Statement of Faith and underline it. ONLY SUCH as are born of the Holy Spirit—and put a circle around that and draw a line between that and your own heart, and you'll be doing something I cannot do for you. Not every one shall enter the kingdom of heaven.

But WE BELIEVE—let's take the WE out and every one from the smallest boy and girl who can say the words to the oldest one—let's take out the word "we" and say—I believe. I believe that the shed blood of Jesus Christ and His resurrection is a sufficient sacrifice for my sins, and I believe in Him, and because I believe in Him, I was born of the Holy Spirit, God has touched my heart and soul and I am not irrevocably lost. I still fail and stumble, but because God has put within my heart something of Himself, I am His child. Will you say that, or will you risk the possibility of being one of those who shall never enter the kingdom of heaven. I believe that the shed blood of Jesus Christ and His resurrection is the basis of my salvation. I believe that, and in the believing of that, something has happened between God and myself, the new birth, conversion, a new experience. I have passed from death into life. And this must happen to every one of you. Don't let anyone ever tell you that a baby can be taken into the kingdom of heaven by someone else. It is a personal responsibility.

Don't fool yourself into thinking that you can live in a Christian home and be part of an evangelical church and be carried along with the crowd. The gate to the kingdom of heaven is wide enough for only one, and when the rest of your family has walked through, you shall present your own credentials.

I don't know about you, but I am so glad that when I come to that solitary spot and stand before Him, I shall have credentials sufficient to gain entrance because I do not come in my own right. I come in the right of the Son of God who loved me and gave Himself for me, and I thank God for the grace of repentance that brought me to accept that. I thank God that He stirred my heart and wounded it until I cried to Him. I thank God that He didn't just let me drift along in my foolishness. I thank God that He brought me up short and brought me to that place where I know in whom I have believed. Strike out the word "we" and say—"I believe—that Jesus died for me."

ARTICLE VII

We believe that water baptism and the Lord's Supper are ordinances to be observed by the Church during the present age. They are, however, not to be regarded as means of salvation.

CHAPTER SEVEN

THE SYMBOLS OF LOVE

Because of misuse of the word "sacrament" in the history of the Church, often the word "ordinance" is used for the Lord's Supper anod baptism. Essentially there is nothing wrong with the word "sacrament" even though it is not a biblical word—in fact, there is no word in the Bible for these two religious rites. They are simply called baptism and the Lord's Supper, and when we seek for a word that expresses both of them, we are forced to take one that is not in the Bible. So it does not dismay us that the word "sacrament" is not biblical —neither is the word "ordinance" except in its inherent meaning.

Originally "sacrament" was a Latin word which simply

meant the binding of a soldier to an oath of obedience. Through the usage of the word in the early church it became a more specific religious rite in which there was divine participation. Essentially "sacrament" means—and this is a pretty good definition of what we mean by "sacrament" or "ordinance"—a holy ordinance instituted by Chirst in which by outward signs the inward grace of God in Christ is represented and sealed to the believer through his participation in faith. If you have that definition, you have a sufficient understanding of what the true spiritual meaning of the sacraments are—the Lord's Supper and baptism.

I will mention in passing that we recognize these two as the only biblical sacraments authorized. The Roman Catholic Church has seven sacraments. The other five are not specifically specified in God's Word, and for this reason the Protestant church ascribes only divine sanction to the two ordinances that Christ Himself administered—Christian baptism and the Lord's Supper.

You will notice in our Statement of Faith there is reference to the ordinances as not being means of salvation. This is very important because many people ascribe to a sacrament an automatic grace of God which is not really there, as if there were some magic way in which someone can be taken into God's grace through the outward application of water or can be forgiven of their sin through the eating and drinking of physical elements. There is no automatic grace of God in the elements or in the sacrament itself. This ought to be obvious from Scripture, and yet it has been the cause of much misunderstanding. The grace of the sacrament is linked to the Word of God and to the faith of the one who participates. As we discuss each one of these, baptism and the Lord's Supper, we shall see clearly why this is true.

The essential meaning of baptism is, first of all, purification. We are going to check some Scripture references in order that you might understand from God's Word what is the meaning of baptism. Ezekiel 36:25 speaks of cleansing on the part of one who is sprinkled or washed with water. This is in a passage in Ezekiel which speaks of a new covenant in which the heart shall be cleansed and there shall be a symbol of that cleansing. "I will sprinkle clean water upon you, and you shall be clean from all your uncleanness and from all your idols I will cleanse you." In Titus 3:5 we have another reference to the purification that baptism represents, "He saved us not because of deeds done by us in righteousness but in virtue of his own mercy by the washing of regeneration and renewal in the Holy Spirit which he poured out upon us richly through Jesus Christ our Savior." Then in the book of Hebrews, chapter 10, verse 22, "Let us draw near with a true heart in full assurance of faith with our hearts sprinkled clean from an evil conscience and our bodies washed with pure water."

Now the reference here to purification and washing is absolutely essential to the understanding of baptism. Baptism is not simply some arbitrary way of representing salvation, it is a very meaningful symbolism that when the body is washed with water there is a cleansing of outward dirt. This is to represent that when Jesus Christ through His grace cleanses the heart there is a purification process. Lest anyone misunderstand this and think that by simply applying water and cleansing the outer body something miraculous takes place in which the heart is cleansed from sin, he ought to understand that the Scripture very clearly teaches that this is not true. In I Peter 3:21 Peter is speaking of the analogy of Noah and the flood and God's salvation, "Baptism which corresponds to this now saves you, not as the removal of dirt from the body, but as an appeal to God for a clear conscience through the resurrection of Jesus Christ." Now this is so obvious that there ought to be no misunderstanding, that it is not the application of water on the body that cleanses the heart from sin. Without a conscience toward God baptism is a meaningless and empty representation.

This leads us to the second aspect of baptism, and that is not only purification but identification. We find this thought in Romans 6. Many times identification is made the primary meaning of baptism. This is not so. Baptism is to represent inward purification through cleansing, but it also represents the identification of the individual with Christ. Hear these words from Romans 6:3. "Do you not know you who have been baptized into Christ Jesus were baptized into his death. We were buried therefore with him by baptism into death, so that as Christ was raised from the dead by the glory of the Father, we too might walk in newness of life." Col. 2:12 also speaks of being buried with Christ in baptism and being raised with Him in His resurrection. Thus in our baptism there is an identification made between us and Jesus Christ in His death and resurrection, and this is very important—the cleansing of our heart is not simply the desire that we have but it is the work of Christ on the cross and there is identification on our part with what Christ has done for us.

This is why baptism is always a public confession of faith in Christ. There is no intimation of anything else in Scripture. Baptism is not to be done secretly or covertly, and if baptism is sought as a private confirmation of one's forgiveness of sin, it has lost its meaning, because baptism is to be seen. It is to be a public identification of the believer with Jesus Christ. If we would understand this, it would keep us from the error that baptism is a means of grace that is not available through simple faith in Jesus Christ. Baptism is not indispensable to the kingdom of God. Baptism is not a prerequisite to entering the kingdom of God. Baptism is not the portal through which we enter the kingdom of God. Baptism is the answer of the conscience that has been cleansed from its sin in a public way of identification that it is through the work of Christ that this is possible.

You will note that our Statement of Faith makes no reference to the age of the subjects for baptism. This is important because in the Evangelical Free Church we believe that our Statement of Faith ought to be limited to defining in a positive way the irreducible minimum of Christian theology. It is not our purpose to separate Christians into one category or another. The question of who is a legitimate subject for baptism is simply a way of stating the problem of infant baptism as against believers' baptism. According to our Statement of Faith there is no reason why an infant cannot be baptized. It does not forbid it. On the other hand, we are unashamed of what we do believe concerning the meaning of baptism. The Scripture nowhere makes a direct reference to the baptism of infants, neither does it forbid it. Those who baptize infants are not going against the express command of Scripture. If we accept the fact that there is no grace of God involved apart from the participation of the individual, it does seem to make the baptism of infants rather pointless, even though harmless. We are not in the business of discriminating against the practice of different modes of baptism or different subjects for baptism.

Baptism is only this, it is a representation of the inward grace of God in the heart by which the sins are cleansed through Christ's death, and it is the identification of the individual in the work of Christ on the cross. That's very simple, isn't it? There ought not to be any quarrels over the meaning of baptism if we recognize that the body of Christ is one, and with that premise we take our stand and in a positive way teach that baptism is not a prerequisite to the kingdom of God—it is a Christian responsibility of those who know Jesus Christ and can give profession of faith in Him.

Now for a few words on the Lord's Supper. You remember, of course, the words of institution came at the time of the last supper that Jesus Christ had with His disciples. There is an account of this in Matthew, Mark, and Luke. In I Cor. 11 Paul gives us the only other account of the institution of the Lord's Supper. The Lord's Supper ought to be the one place where God's people can find a common fellowship, and if there is one thing that is distressing to me it is the fact that there are so many who make the Lord's table the place of division. In all of the talk of ecumenicity, that is, the gathering together of all the churches into one organization, it is an appalling thing to me that when they have their conferences the one thing they always make sure is that the various denominations can have separate communion services. The Lord's table is the one place where there is no hierarchy and where there is one fellowship.

The elements of the Lord's table are the common elements of the table fare of His day. When Jesus participated in the last supper they were eating bread and they were drinking wine, and these were on the table of every Hebrew of that day. He did not introduce some foreign element, but He took thos things which were already a part of their life and He sanctified them through His own memory. We do this every day— we take things which are common to other people, and in a relationship of love and friendship we sanctify them with a peculiar significance to ourselves, and they become symbols of love. And we are not fooled for a moment, thinking that these symbols are somehow changed into something else—how preposterous! The meaning of the symbols is that which is invested upon them by the heart concerned. Jesus took the bread and wine and said—now, when you participate in this again, you remember who I am. Don't forget me—remember that my body will be broken on the cross, and when you eat the broken bread do not forget that. Remember that my blood shall pour from my veins and I shall give my life as a sacrifice for your sins, and when you drink of the cup remember this. Remember what a bond there is between us—do this in memory of me.

In I Cor. 11 Paul warns against the misuse of the symbols of love. He says in verse 28, "Let a man examine himself"— and when we issue an invitation to the Lord's table we issue it to the children of God who by their own profession of faith in Christ come at Christ's invitation. Let a man examine himself. Paul goes on to say that he that eats and drinks without discerning the Lord's body brings damnation upon himself, and this teaches us that the Lord's table is a fellowship in which the Lord's body is to be discerned. And what IS the Lord's body? It is the Church—and when we sit at the Lord's table we dare not sit isolated from each other. We are to participate in this sacrament with a sense of community life with each other, and this also is why the sacrament of the Lord's Supper has no meaning when it is administered in solitude, because it is a corporate thing; and whenever the Lord's Supper as a sacrament is privately administered apart from the communal life of the church it is in danger of becoming a personal means of salvation or assurance. The Scripture does not forbid this, but there is danger here of taking something which binds us together and using it as a personal means of acquiring divine grace.

Let me remind you of two or three things. First, a sacrament is *only spiritual if it is personal*. The relationship between husband and wife is an analogy. If a husband and wife participate in some symbolic act with each other and there is no personal involvement, it is just a form. You and I both know it is meaningless. A sacrament is only spiritual if it is personal. And God is a person, and the sacrament of baptism and the sacrament of the Lord's Supper involve a personal relationship with God. If there is no personal relationship it is not spiritual. Whenever you participate in a communion service and there is no personal relationship in your heart between you and God, there is no spiritual reality involved, whether it's baptism or the Lord's Supper.

Second, *every personal relationship demands symbolized communion*. Whether it's a handshake between friends, whether it is written words that convey the meaning of who we are and what we are doing to each other, whether it is the physical relationship in marriage, which becomes a spiritual act if there is personal involvement, every personal relationship *demands* a symbolized communion. And every relationship of the individual with God demands a symbolized communion, because this is who we are. And yet how many of you ignore the fact that your relationship with God demands a symbolized communion.

We have our communion service on Wednesday evening and the attendance has never been more than one-third of the Sunday morning attendance. There are some who have suggested that if we bring our communion service to the Sunday morning service, we shall triple our attendance, and that is obvious. How do you explain your absence from the Lord's table when every personal relationship demands a symbolized communion. Don't tell me it's because you cannot work it into your schedule—I refuse to accept that. Tell me it's inconvenient and you will be giving the right answer. Tell your heart it is inconvenient to participate in a symbolized communion of your relationship with Jesus Christ. The fact that there is only one-third of you who attend the communion service indicates that the two-thirds of you have very little personal relationship with God. How do you explain your absence from the communion table? I have little interest in bringing communion to you, to hide your inconvenience in participation.

Without love the symbols of love are not only empty but dangerous. They give false security, and there are far more people who have been baptized as infants who think they have a passport to heaven than there are who look upon their baptism as a personal spiritual testimony. Without love the symbols of love are not only empty, but they are dangerous because they lead to a process of insensitivity. Every time you participate in a symbol of love without there being love you are hardening your heart, and this is why you can participate in the Lord's Supper, or take communion as you call it, and get up and have the same hostility and unlove in your heart as when you sat down.

The matter that concerns me is this—do you love the Lord? Do you? Is there anything in your heart of personal love for Jesus Christ? I mean to take away from you the sacraments until you can take them for yourselves. I mean to strip from you the security of simply being baptized as if this somehow brought you into the kingdom. I mean to take from you the convenience of sitting at the Lord's table until you come of your own choosing. Do you really love the Lord—do you understand that this is the only thing that really matters, and that if Jesus Christ were here this morning, He would not simply give you communion—He would probe your heart and your life for response. He would look into your eyes and say —who ARE you? Are you a disciple, a believer, are you committed? Are you a Christian? He would not allow you to evade.

I only care that you love the Lord and that this love is a matter of your personal confession of faith in Christ and of your life for Him; and if you do and if you have not been baptized I shall someday stand with you and I shall hear your testimony that you do love the Lord and you shall be baptized as a public confession of faith in Jesus Christ. And if you do love the Lord today, next communion service I shall sit with you at the Lord's table, and your chair shall not be empty and our hearts shall be strengthened by our mutual participation in who Christ is.

ARTICLE VIII

We believe that the true Church is composed of all such persons who through saving faith in Jesus Christ have been regenerated by the Holy Spirit and are united together in the body of Christ of which He is the Head.

CHAPTER EIGHT

THE CHURCH—A BELIEVING COMMUNITY

The minute we mention the word "church" we are faced with a multitude of thoughts and speculations as to the nature of the Church. In theology this is known as ecclesiology—the doctrine of the Church. The Greek word which is translated "church" in our Bibles is *ekklesia* and it technicaly means a called assembly. The word was familiar in the time of the New Testament before the time of Christ and was in common use for any group called through proclamation, perhaps a civil group, perhaps a community group. But the word has taken on a technical meaning in the New Testament because the *ekklesia* is a called assembly of God's own people, through the call of Jesus Christ in the human heart.

THE CHURCH—A BELIEVING COMMUNITY

When we speak of the "Church" we speak of many things. If you were to visit someone's home this afternoon, they might ask you—did you go to church today?—indicating by that remark that the church is a place. If you talk with someone who is unacquainted with you, they might ask you—are you a member of the church?—indicating that the church is some kind of organization to which you might belong. There was a time on a particular Saturday when some of you said—I am going to work on the church today—and you would take your hammer and saw and leave home. Now what are you working on when you are working on the church, do you know? What is the Church? There was a time a few years ago when a few of you said—we are going to start a church here in Covina. How do you start a church? Do you take two sticks and rub them together until there's a flame? Is it like kindling a fire? Do you start a church by buying a church mix—you know, a box with all the ingredients in it and you just add water? How do you start a church? What *is* a church?

Isn't it strange how easily we use this word and tie it into our conversation, yet none of the specific references are really the Church. The Church is not the building which we build with hammer and saw, the Church is not the organization that is represented by our membership list, the Church is not this plot of ground on which you park your car and tarry for a moment.

What is the Church? Our Statement of Faith attempts to set forth for us in clear terms the distinctive of the Church, and Christians, or even non-Christians, ought to understand what the Church is and what it is not. There is an interesting reference found in Acts 20:28 which helps us clear away the debris of what a church is not. Paul is here speaking to the Ephesian church and he says, "Take heed to yourselves and to all the flock, in which the Holy Spirit has made you guardians, to feed the church of the Lord, which he obtained with his own blood." Now whatever the Church is, it was purchased with blood. And what will blood buy? Human souls, nothing else. So that the Church essentially must be something which can be purchased with blood. It must be persons, human souls. In Col. 4:15 Paul makes a passing reference to a woman named Nympha and the church in her house, and from this we understand that that which can be purchased with blood has to be a person but that the person is more than one person and is something that can be experienced in a certain place.

The epistle to the Ephesian church is perhaps the finest presentation in the New Testament of the nature and distinctive of the Church of Jesus Christ. There is a word used in the Ephesian epistle in several places which is very significant concerning the nature of the Church as a spiritual reality. In Chapter 1, verse 9, Paul says this, "For he has made known to us in all wisdom and insight the mystery of his will, according to his purpose which he set forth in Christ," and if you will hold the word "mystery" for a moment, we shall see that this is a very important word in the book of Ephesians and an important word concerning what the Church is. In Chapter 2 we do not find a reference to this word "mystery" but in Chapter 3 you shall see the word reappear. Verse 1, "For this reason I, Paul, a prisoner for Christ Jesus on behalf of you Gentiles—assuming that you have heard of the stewardship of God's grace that was given to me for you, how the mystery was made known to me by revelation, as I have written briefly." In other words, he is referring us back to the word used in the first chapter—"the mystery was made known to me by revelation". Paul learned something that no other man knew, and he learned this through a direct revelation of God. The theme of this revelation was the mystery of God's will. Later on in Chapter 3 the word "mystery" is used again. Verse 9, "And to make all men see what is the plan of the mystery hidden for ages in God who created all things." And in verse 10 is the explanation of the mystery, "That through the church the manifold wisdom of God might now be made known to the principalities and powers in the heavenly places. This was according to the eternal purpose which he has realized in Christ Jesus our Lord." So that the Church is the mystery of God's wisdom and will.

Now why should there have been a mystery concerning God's purpose? The mystery of God's purpose is God's intention beyond Israel. When God carefully taught Israel to separate themselves from the Gentiles and to prove their exclusiveness through specific religious rites and taught them that they were superior not because of who they were but because they had a distinct and personal relationship to God, what did God have in mind? The Jews thought that because of this exclusiveness they must be an exclusive people and they thought perhaps God had selected them because of their own merits. That wasn't true. The mystery of what God had in mind was that through the Church the whole world should be brought within the scope of redemptive grace. The Church is a continuing revelation of the sacred purpose of God's life, that through Jesus Christ would come an access into the kingdom of God for all people, every race, every nation and tribe on earth. In verse 6 of Ephesians 3 this is very clearly specified, "that is, how the Gentiles are fellow heirs, members of the same body, and partakers of the promise in Christ Jesus through the gospel."

You must know this, that the Church is not an accident, nor is it an innovation. The Church was in God's mind from the beginning, because it was the way in which the gospel of Jesus Christ would encompass the whole world, and we are part of something that God is now revealing to all men.

Let us move rather quickly into the nature of the Church as a spiritual reality. Just what is the Church as you and I experience it? You will note in our Statement of Faith several things: first of all, the word "regenerated" is used to indicate that only those regenerated by the Holy Spirt comprise the essence of the Church. Now this simply means that the Church has a common baptism, one baptism. In I Cor. 12:13, "For by one spirit we were all baptized into one body—Jews or Greeks, slaves or free—and all were made to drink of one Spirit." We normally think of baptism as a sacrament of the Church, but there is only one baptism, the various modes of baptism notwithstanding, and that one baptism is that spiritual baptism by which a work of grace takes place in the human heart and the individual is baptized into a fellowship. The individual is baptized into this fellowship by the direct work of the Holy

Spirit in his heart. Regeneration is only a technical term for this new birth which is always individual and is always spiritual and is always a supernatural divine work. Thus the Church is not of human origin, but of divine; and we can't any more build a church here in this sense than we can save men ourselves from their sins. The only thing we can do to start a church is to first recognize that God has worked in our hearts and that we are born again and that we have been baptized into a greater fellowship than just human existence. Because of this, wherever we recognize God's grace in another, there the Church is coming into existence. So to start a church is simply to recognize that God is dwelling in certain lives, and when those lives come together and begin an organizational life, the Church becomes focused on one place.

New birth is the growth of the Church, and when we speak of our church growing, we are only saying that regeneration is taking place. It is not that we have a recruitment program by which we are building membership of the church, but that we have a program of recognition and a ministry of repentance and faith, and that wherever God has worked in the human heart the Church is growing. Of course if God is not at work the Church is not growing, and we can fill every seat in this building and build other buildings; but if God is not at work in human hearts to transform them and regenerate them from darkness into light, the Church is not growing.

There is a common baptism, and there is a communal life. Did you note the phrase in the Statement of Faith that they are "united together"—those who are regenerated by the Holy Spirit are united together into a fellowship, a believing community. There is no such thing as a solitary Christian. It's an impossible concept, because a solitary Christian is always a member of something greater than himself. To become a Christian is to be baptized by the Holy Spirit through regeneration into a fellowship. Only sinners are solitary, that is what sin is. Only unbelief is alone. There is no fellowship in a cemetery because everyone is dead, there is no fellowship in sinners because sinners are cubicles of isolation; and so to speak of a solitary Christian is a contradiction in terms. You might as well say an unbelieving Christian. Now there are some Christians who prefer to be left alone, but they are going against their own relationships. There are some members of a family who prefer to be left alone, they don't want to talk with any one, they prefer to be in their own room all the time; but there's something wrong with that family unit. That's not the way it ought to be.

There's a beautiful expression in Scripture of the Church and that is the "household of faith". In Galatians 6:10 you have it, also Ephesians 2:19. Galatians 6:10 says, "So then, as we have opportunity, let us do good to all men, and especially to those who are of the household of faith." Now a household is a family unit—it's a group of people who have a communal life, who share certain things in common that no one else shares with them.

Turn back to the second chapter of Acts, the very birthplace of the Church itself. After the Day of Pentecost when the Holy Spirit came, an unmistakable sign that the human heart was regenerated and God's power was now in the human life—on that day when many people were brought into the kingdom through the baptism of the Holy Spirit, we find that they recognized immediately the communal life that they shared. They devoted themselves to three things, Acts 2:42, ". . . the apostles' teaching and fellowship, to the breaking of bread and the prayers." The word fellowship is not just a social time together, they didn't have a coffee break at the end of every session. The technical word for fellowship is *koinonia* and that which is *koinos* is common, it's not esoteric, it's not exclusive, it's not exotic, it's common, that which is known and shared and participated in by everyone. So that *koinonia* is the common life we have together because of certain things. First, there is recognition in each other of the new life. There is rcognition in each other of the same basic need of each other and contribution to each other's life. This is why they devoted themselves not only to the doctrinal teaching of God's Word, the Gospel, but they devoted themselves to the *koinonia*, the household of faith, and they worked just as hard at expressing who they were with each other as they did at learning why they were children of God and what the Gospel of Christ was. The *koinonia* is important. Without *koinonia* the church is dead.

We have had individuals who have entered into our fellowship in the past two or three years, and they have discovered that you cannot remain anonymous in our fellowship—well, I should hope not. I would hope that there is not one of your households where a person could enter and live for three weeks and no one would know his name. What a terrible thing! I should hope that this would be the kind of fellowship where it would be impossible to remain anonymous. Ah, but you recognize that many people prize anonymity, and they would say—we have come to worship God, not to be discovered. And we must insert at this point that it is impossible to be a solitary Christian. It is impossible to have a healthy spiritual life and to be anonymous. Now there are places where anonymity is grouped together, and it is those places that become a haven for these souls who cannot bear the intimacy of God's people who recognize each other, because with recognition comes expectation and revelation. But with recognition also comes acceptance and security and love.

For the few people who have said—you cannot be anonymous here, we shall have to leave—there have been a score who have entered in and said—this is a place where love is real; this is a place where we not only worship God in a singleness of heart, but this is a place where the reality of God's love and grace is experienced with each other; it is a place where our hearts can be filled with mutual friendship; it is a place where we exhort one another by our joint commitment to the gospel of Christ; it is a place where when one falls, another strengthens him; it is a place where when one falters, another reaches out a hand; it is a place where if one heart becomes barren and empty, another heart shares its joy; it is a place where no tear drops unwatched; it is a place where no grief is shared in solitude—this is the church. It is a real thing. It's a place that can meet not only man's basic spiritual need of being forgiven from sin, but it can meet the total emotional and social needs of the individual. It has always been thus—God's people are a household of faith, a family, and a fellowship. Those who have been regenerated by the Holy Spirit are united together in the *koinonia,* and this is the Church.

But there's something else—the body of Christ. In Ephesians 1, verses 22 and 23, we have this phrase, "He has put all things under his feet and has made him the head over all things for the church, which is his body." Eph. 5:23, "For the husband is the head of the wife as Christ is the head of the church, his body, and is himself its Savior." Now what is a body, would you tell me? What is your body for? Could you be who you are without a body? Well, you would say—yes, because essentially I am a spirit, and my spirit is my real self. What do you use your body for? The body is the expression of the person. If we didn't have bodies, we wouldn't recognize each other, would we? If these chairs were all empty and there was no one standing up here, no body, we wouldn't know we were here. We couldn't shake hands—we wouldn't have any hands. We couldn't see each other, couldn't hear each other, couldn't touch each other, we couldn't do anything if we didn't have bodies. You see how important the body is. It's the expression of who we are—not only for our own sakes (can you imagine looking in the mirror with no body?) but it's the expression of who we are with each other—recognition, sharing, touching, assurance.

Now what relationship does my body have to who I am? My total self is not expressed completely through just one part of my body. You've heard the expression—he has more talent in his little finger than I have in my whole body. Well, that may be true of talent, but it takes all ten of my fingers and both eyes and ears to totally express who I am, and yet any one part of my body is just as much me. If I cut my finger, I say—I hurt. Or I might say—my finger hurts. You say—cut it off if it hurts, and I'd say—then my hand would hurt. Cut your hand off—my arm would hurt then. What we are really saying is that I hurt if any part of me hurts. A body is a wonderful thing, absolutely important.

Now if the Church is the body of Christ, what is it? If the Church has the same relationship to Jesus Christ as my body to my spirit, what is the Church other than the necessary expression of Christ Himself? You treat a member of the body with cruelty and the person suffers. You treat one member of the Church of Jesus Christ with cruelty and hostility, and who suffers—Jesus Christ. But, you say, it's just one person. Ah, but it's a part of the body, and the body is only an expression of who God is. Do you realize what a church is? A church is the expression of God in a tangible form, the only tangible expression of God is the composite divinity of the Church. Every member of the Church put together represents the complete identification of God in the world through Jesus Chirst. Is it any wonder that Paul said, "You are the temple of the Holy Spirit and God dwells in you." Is it any wonder that Paul said with reverent language, "We are built upon the foundation of the apostles and prophets, Christ Jesus himself being the cornerstone, in whom the whole structure is joined together and grows into a holy temple in the Lord, in whom you also are built into it for a dwelling place of God in the Spirit." (Eph. 2:20-22)

If God dwells in the Church, and the Church is nothing more than a wrangling body of cantankerous souls, is this who God is? If God dwells in the Church and the Church is nothing more than a group of competitive individuals who are trying to outdo one another, is this who God is? We have many moments we are not proud of, but we have many moments together in which we recognize that it is none other than God Himself working in our hearts, when in spite of ourselves we love, when in spite of who we are, there is a redemptive therapy that takes place in our midst. And this is where God dwells—in the hearts of people.

A little boy came home from Sunday School, which took place in a large church at the same time as the morning worship service and he got mixed up. He came home and told his daddy—Daddy, I went into the big church this morning—and his daddy was horrified and said—not all the way in, I hope—and the boy said—how do you go just part way into a church. Of course, you don't; and this is why you are either in the Church or you're not—you're not just part way in. You

THE CHURCH—A BELIEVING COMMUNITY

have either been baptized in through a work of God's grace through the Holy Spirit in your heart, or you are still outside. You are either part of the *koinonia* that is our fellowship, or you see it from outside and are impressed by it but are not part of it. How does one become a member of the body of Christ? God has taken care of that. He will work in your heart to forgive your sins and through a spiritual and supernatural work God Himself will come to dwell in your life, and when that happens you are part of the Church of Christ.

ARTICLE IX

We believe that only those who are thus members of the true Church shall be eligible for membership in the local church.

CHAPTER NINE

THE CHURCH—A COMMITTED COMMUNITY

It has long been the custom of those who wish to distinguish between the body of Christ and the church as a local fellowship to use the terminology "visible" and "invisible" church, stating that the body of Christ essentially is the invisible church and that the local congregation is the visible church. This is not altogether a satisfactory distinction, because we all too frequently give greater value to that which is visible, and it would seem that we are trying to separate that which naturally belongs together. In reality the body always has its temporal manifestations in this life, so when we speak of the invisible church as an entity by itself, we are rupturing the body. It's like trying to speak of a person as only a spirit, and that's impossible. A person is more than spirit, a person is spirit and body.

It is much better if we speak of the body of Christ as both a communion of believers and a community of believers, and that the body in this sense has both communion and commitment. When we have used the word "communion" we are speaking of the spiritual reality that binds us together in one organism, the body of Christ; and when we speak of community we speak of the working, temporal, organizational fellowship, the committed community. The first, the communion of believers, is a spiritual calling through regeneration. The second, the community of believers, is a voluntary commitment in recognition that there is already spiritual communion.

Now the Statement of Faith simply says that the membership among the community of believers is only legitimate for those who are already partaking of the spiritual communion of believers. In amplification of this, I would like to clarify what we as a church mean when we speak of church membership. I think it would be well for us to clarify in our own thinking our relationship both to the communion of believers through the spiritual calling of regeneration and the community of believers. Do we belong any place? Do we have a household of faith?

First, we suggest that membership is a recognition of the body of Christ. Now this would be obvious, I think, if we would accept the statement that first of all there must be a communion of believers before there can be a community of believers. In accepting members into a community of believers we are only recognizing that the body of Christ comes into existence through the spiritual calling of regeneration. Whenever I talk with anyone I've asked to join our church, I make it very clear that becoming a member of a church, a local congregation, is not the conferring of any spiritual status. It is not the granting of a spiritual diploma, it is not elevation into some spiritual degree, it is only our recognition of the fact that you are already in the Church. It is only the open door into the community of our fellowship, recognizing that you are already a part of our communion in Jesus Christ. This is why we have only one prerequisite for church membership, and that is that the individual give personal testimony to his participation in the communion of believers through personal faith in Jesus Christ.

We move to the next premise which is not stated directly in the Statement of Faith but rather is stated negatively—it says that *only* those who are members of the true Church shall be eligible for membership in the local church. I would like to state it in a positive way as reflecting more the spirit of our fellowship and say—*all* those who are part of the true Church shall be eligible for membership in the local church. And if you're looking for some way to epitomize the distinctive of the Evangelical Free Church, you can state it this way —*all* those who are members of the body of Christ are eligible for membership in the local church. We will set no exclusions where God has opened the door. We believe that the local congregation is to be as open as the kingdom of God itself. Our capacity is not such that we become the judge of the human heart but that we recognize the evidences of a divine work of grace in the human heart, and upon recognition of those evidences we open the door into the community of believers, and we have no right not to open it.

There are many people who as individuals feel unqualified for membership in the local church, and may I speak to such— may I speak words of encouragement and words of expectation. Jesus Christ nowhere indicated that there was to be a probationary period for spiritual communion. The Holy Spirit Himself in a work of grace unites the person immediately into the true communion of believers, and the local congregation has no right to set a probationary period seeking to elevate the spiritual life of the indivdual to make them eligible for membership in the body of Christ. The only important imperative for the local congregation is that it have discernment and clear recognition of the spiritual reality of the indivdual profession of faith.

I have had individuals say to me—I cannot be a member of your church because I smoke. You don't mind my speaking plainly, do you? And I say—how is that—and they reply— I notice most of the people in your church do not smoke, and I personally feel that I can't be a really good Christian as long as I smoke, so I can't be a part of your fellowship. My response to that is—that's strange to me. I hadn't heard of that in our fellowship. Where did you hear that? Well, we just assumed—isn't this what all evangelical churches believe? No, as a matter of fact. And by the way, what is the relationship of one's personal habits which may or may not be immoral to participation in the communion of believers? Let's settle this question. What constitutes participation in the communion of believers? Rebirth through the Holy Spirit. And does the presence of any habit such as gossip, smoking, different types of entertainment—what relationship do these things have to the work of the Holy Spirit as far as qualifications? The answer is —none at all—not directly. We are not to confess the ethical life of the Christian with the prerequisite for membership in the communion of believers. Personally smoke irritates me. If you smoke in my office, the first think I'll do is open the windows and try to get as much air through as I can. It irritates me, and if you smoke in my car, you'll find my ashtray filled with napkins so you can't use it. I don't like to have the windows open for a week afterward to get the smoke out—smoke irritates me. But as far as I am concerned, I can see you through the smoke, and I am sure God can. I don't think God, if He's irritated, is irritated enough to close His eyes to you. God can see you. Now if you don't want to smoke and you want to give it up, give it up for yourself, not for my sake. Don't give up smoking for the sake of our church, we couldn't appreciate it less. And you wouldn't do it very long because you'd resent us for making you do it, wouldn't you? And don't give up smoking for God's sake because you'll end up resenting Him for making you do it. If you're convicted that you should not, give it up for the sake of your own conviction. But whatever the case, don't use this to distort membership in the communion of believers, and don't project upon the community of believers your own insecurities.

I've had people who have been divorced ask me about membership in the local church. That's not the point—the point is, are you a member of the communion of believers? If so, you are eligible for membership. How could we keep you out? On what basis would we make something a stigma and say—you cannot participate in the community of believers though we grant you are a member of the body of Christ. How dare we do that? I want to make it unmistakably clear— if a person belongs to Jesus Christ there are no stigmas attached as far as membership in the community of believers or in this church is concerned. If your moral life needs the strengthening of Christian fellowship, you will find in our church as a member of the community of believers the finest place for it. If you find that your heart needs to be assured that the consequences of some tragedy in your life is not a stigma, where better place can you find than in the community of believers?

There *are* evidences of saving faith, and the first is conversion. In the second chapter of Ephesians Paul says, "And you he made alive when you were dead in trespasses and sins in which you once walked, following the course of this world, following the prince of the power of the air, the spirit that is now at work in the sons of disobedience. Among these we all once lived in the passions of our flesh . . ." Conversion is simply a turning away from the world and all of its downward tendencies into the kingdom of God with all of its edifying tendencies. Conversion is the human aspect of the regeneration that the Holy Spirit does in the heart, and when we look for evidences of new birth we look for conversion first. Secondly, we look for testimony. "He who believes in the Son of God has the testimony in himself" (I John 5:10).

When your children ask to become members of our church, we are interested in only one thing—are they members of the communion of believers? We don't ask how old they are, we don't ask how many Scriptures verses they have memorized, we don't make them promise anything; we only want to know —are they members of the communion of believers, and there's only one way to determine that; first, through conversion, and second, through testimony. He who is a member of the communion of believers has a testimony in himself, and your sons and daughters will give testimony before our deacon board of their own personal faith in Jesus Christ. We will not call you in and have you speak for them—is that all right? "He that believes in the Son of God has the testimony in himself"—and we accept that for what it is. We take your word for it, because your testimony is not only what you dare to say but what you dare to be.

Finally, the evidence of saving faith is fellowship—one in heart. In Ephesians 4:3 we read it, "Eager to maintain the unity of the Spirit in the bond of peace. There is one body and one Spirit." There is a way of recognition of those who belong to Jesus Christ. These are the things that we use in recogniton of those who are members of the communion of believers, and we say—welcome to the community of believers, our local congregation.

Membership is not only recognition of the body of Christ, it is an organizaton of spiritual unity. By the word "organization" I mean the bringing together and effectualizing of the spiritual unity that exists in Christ. Did you notice in verse 3 of Ephesians 4, "Eager to maintain the unity of the Spirit in the bond of peace." Now the bond of peace is the community of believers. The bond of peace is that which holds us together in an organizational fellowship so that we can maintain the unity of the Spirit. The unity of the Spirit without the bond of peace will soon be dissolved and lost through individualism and subjectivism.

A community is no stronger than its organized unity, whether it's a family community, a national community, a neighborhood community, or a Christian community. The fellowship of believers is no stronger than its organized unity. This involves a determined constituency, a household of faith. We know who is in the household and who is not, and this is necessary for the strength of the community. This demands a common rule. In Eph. 5:21 Paul says, "Be subject to one another out of reverence for Christ." Communal life requires subjection to one another and requires a common rule. In our families we have unity through birth and marriage. The family is first of all a family because it has a communion, but this communion, this unity, would not last very long without down-to-earth harmony. This is why we try our best to eat our meals all together, we try our best to all sleep at night and be awake in the daytime. I say we try our best—it's not always possible. We try our best to have a semblance of community harmony as an affirmation of our communion with each other as members of the family.

Some say they do not agree with the way the church is run so they cannot be a member of it, and I say—fine, then find one where you can agree. And if you can't, then something is wrong, because there's only one question you must ask and that is—is God at work in any specific Christian community, by that, I mean a local congregation. Is God at work in our fellowship? Is He? If He is, then how come He's not as fussy as you are? Do you realize that if you cannot agree with the way our church is run and thus you cannot be a member of it and yet you have to confess that God is working here, then you have greater scruples than God. That's what it amounts to—because God has this wonderful quality about Him, He requires only honesty, not perfection, and He'll work where there are honest hearts.

People have left our church and told me they couldn't quite agree with what has been said and done and so they were going to try and find a church more in accord with their own beliefs, and I have said—fine, but you realize there are two problems involved. First, there is the problem of who *we* are—apparently there is something lacking. The second problem is who you are, and you're going to take that with you. You'll leave us with our problems. I would invite you to stay and help us work them out; I would invite you to stay and help this church become what you think a church should be. That's the only way it will.

Thank God for those who do stay. Thank God for those who recognize God is working here, and through their work they shall make this fellowship into a church that is a credit to Jesus Christ and a fulfillment of His ministry. Some wait until a church reveals its direction before they commit themselves to it. This does two things: first, it robs the church of vitally needed help in a time of new growth; and second, it disintegrates the individual's spiritual life. You canot wait around very long without losing out spiritually.

The Church is not only a recognition of the body of Christ, an organization of spiritual unity; the church is a spiritual fellowship that through organization accomplishes spiritual things. Is organization itself unspiritual? Of course not. Those who resist organization are attempting to justify their own rebellion. In a community of believers, unaffiliation is always a form of irresponsibility—always. In a neighborhood community, unaffiliation is irresponsibility; in a family community, unaffiliation is irresponsibility; and in a church community, unaffiliation is irresponsibility. Not rebellion, but irresponsibility—the unwillingness to say—count on me, whether it's good or bad I'm a part of it. And this is the test of the unity that builds churches. Eph. 4:12-13 tells us that gifts were given to the Church "for the equipment of the saints, for the work of ministry, for building up the body of Christ, until we all attain to the unity of the faith and of the knowledge of the Son of God, to mature manhood, to the measure of the stature of the fulness of Christ."

I would suggest to you finally that membership in a church is a confession of mutual need and that the church is not a reward for virtue, but it is a refuge for the desperate. It's a place where we come together in recognition of our immaturity, and through fellowship we struggle for personal maturity and mutual maturity. If it is easy to join a community of believers through membership, it is easier not to; and one of the reasons it is easier not to is that we do not beg you to. We will allow you the luxury of being a part of the communion of believers without necessarily being a part of the community of believers. We will allow that—but every communion expects a commitment. A boy and girl going together for a long period of time might have wonderful communion, but sooner or later she's going to wonder when the date is going to be set, isn't she? And if he responds and says—well, why do we need to set a date, don't we love each other, isn't this enough? The answer is—no, it isn't. Communion without commitment is insufficient.

This is why church membership is the fulfillment of expectation, mutual expectation.

Every believer is part of the communion of the body of Christ. Church membership is not discrimination. Every believer has an invitation to membership in the community of Christ's body, and this invitation is always open. Several times during the year we make it clear we are having instruction classes for those who are seeking membership in our church to orient them regarding the constitution of our church and what we mean by church membership. Many times I will speak to individuals and suggest it would be helpful to them to affiliate themselves. I trust I have never been guilty of forcing anyone into membership.

Acts 9:26 speaks of Paul shortly after his conversion, "And when he had come to Jerusalem he attempted to join the disciples." Thank God for that spirit. But here's an interesting thing. "They were all afraid of him, for they did not believe that he was a disciple." I am happy to say that we have not had to be afraid of any one who has sought fellowship with us. I am happy to say we have not had to turn anyone away because we didn't believe he was a disciple.

But what happened to Paul, do you know? A man by the name of Barnabas, verse 27, "Took him and brought him to the apostles, and declared to them how on the road he had seen the Lord, who spoke to him, and how at Damascus he had preached boldly in the name of Jesus." Barnabas took him and led him into the fellowship. We need Barnabas today as much as we need Paul. We need a Barnabas to take someone and encourage him to become a member of the community of believers. Perhaps you could be a Barnabas. Perhaps you don't need to wait for Barnabas. In any event, the Spirit of God must lead you. This is the church. A communion of believers who are committed with each other in a community of believers, both the body of Jesus Christ.

ARTICLE X

We believe that Jesus Chirst is the Lord and Head of the Church and that every local church has the right under Christ to decide and govern its own affairs.

CHAPTER TEN

THE CHURCH—A DISCIPLINED COMMUNITY

This statement is a logical inference drawn from the biblical premise that the Church in every manifestation is complete because the body is one. If the local congregation is a complete manifestation of the body of Christ, then Jesus Christ who is the head of the Church is the head of the local congregation and the relationship of the local congregation is one of supreme allegiance to Jesus Christ directly.

Perhaps an example will help. Humanity is more than one man because humanity is as extensive as every man, but every man is a complete representative of humanity. Two men do not increase the depth of humanity; when you have one man, you have the total dimension of humanity in that one person. This is the way it is with the body of Christ. The local congregation is as a man is to humanity—the local congregation is all of the Church that there is. Two churches do not make more Church any more than two men make more man except from the standpoint of the mutual strength involved and mutual encouragement. There is a relationship between men, but it is a fraternal one, not the relationship of a part to a whole. Each man is a complete dimension of humanity. Likewise, each congregation is a complete dimension of the Church though it has a fraternal relationship with other churches even as a man has a fraternal relationship with other men.

I Corinthians 12 is often used to show that there is a relationship between churches as the relationship of the members of a person's body to the body itself. "For just as the body is one and has many members, and all the members of the body, though many, are one body, so it is with Christ." (I Cor. 12:12) Here the members are not individual churches which comprise one body. The members are the individuals within the body of Christ who are represented to comprise the total body. We could lead our discussion one step further by asking this question, "Is one person the Church?" We would have to say no, because one person is only a member of the body of Christ, one person is not the body. There is the body of Christ and there are members, and the members are individuals who are placed in the body of Christ through a spiritual birth. Verse 13, "For by one Spirit we were all baptized into one body —Jews or Greeks, slaves or free—and all were made to drink of one Spirit." This is why the Church requires at least two members because of the concept of the body having several members. How large is the Church then? The Church is as large as the members of the body of Jesus Christ, and wherever you find an individual who through relationship with Jesus Christ has been born again, you find a member of the Church. Now you may be Presbyterian, Methodist, Baptist, or Evangelical Free—this is immaterial to membership in the body of Christ, as we so often emphasize.

What then is the meaning of Jesus Christ being the head of the body when the body is more than a local congregation? The local congregation is only a representative manifestation of the body; it is never the complete body in the sense that our local congregation is all the Church there is any more than one man is all of the humans that there are. We are sufficient in our body to be the total dimension of the Church of Christ, but we do not claim to be the only manifestation.

What do we mean when we speak of the body of Christ and the headship of Jesus Christ over the local congregation? You will note in the Statement of Faith that there is a slightly argumentative tone—"Every church has the right under Christ to decide and govern its own affairs". It sounds almost as if we were taking back something that had been taken away from us, and that is precisely true. If you understand the heritage of our Evangelical Free Church, you will understand something of the nature of this Statement of Faith, for this truth was rescued from those who said that the local congregation is only a part of a larger ecclesiastical body who makes the decisions. You must understand something of the nature of the churches in Scandinavia where the Evangelical Free Church had its origin. Even today Norway and Sweden have a State Church. This means that the government of the country taxes every citizen of the country to support the ministers and the churches, and that the king himself is the one who determines ultimately the procedures and policies of the State Church.

Now there were within this structure those who saw the distortion of this, and lest I be too harsh here, let me remind you there are abuses in every form of church government. But there were abuses in this form of church government and those within the structure said—this cannot be the Church of Jesus Christ—and they searched the Scriptures and found that if you met in a fellowship in a home and believed in Jesus Christ, you were the Church, and they dared to believe this. They paid their taxes which went toward the support of the State Church, they were not rebels or anarchists, but they said —we have the right to say that our meeting is a true church— and they rescued the church from this structure which had become a tyranny and not a church. They met in their homes for spiritual fellowship, they supported their own missionaries, and they had a concept that the Church is primarily an organism and only secondarily an organization. When these inspired people immigrated to America, there was one thing they were going to be sure of, and that was to protect that which they had rescued. So for a number of years they resisted any attempts at organization, but they found as we all find that organization is not an enemy of the organism, the body had to be coordinated, and as long as the organism is given priority, the organization is a fine thing. So they organized in one sense as the Evangelical Free Church, and we have a common origin with many other groups. This explains our own background, and thus you understand the wording, "Every local church has the right under Christ to decide and govern its own affairs."

Let us turn to the authority of the Church and discuss it under three basic headings: first, the spiritual rule of the Church. Here we are simply going to draw out some of the implications we've already made, the principle that Jesus Christ is the head of the Church. Let us trace in the Scriptures this truth. We shall begin with Eph. 1:22, which is Paul's way of clarifying the relationship of Jesus Christ to the Church. "And he (that is, God) has put all things under his feet (that is, Christ) and has made him the head over all things for the church, which is his body, the fulness of him who fills all in all." In Eph. 2:20, "Members of the household of God, built upon the foundation of the apostles and prophets, Christ Jesus himself being the cornerstone, in whom the whole structure is is joined together and grows into a holy temple in the Lord; in whom you also are built into it for a dwelling place of God in the Spirit." This is why those folks meeting in their homes without stained glass windows, without liturgy, without hymn books, dared to believe that they were the dwelling place of God, that they were built into a structure that could not be seen but nonetheless was real, and that Jesus Christ Himself was the cornerstone, and they said—we are complete in Him. We are a complete body of Christ.

In Eph. 5:21-24, "Be subject to one another out of reverence for Christ. Wives, be subject to your husbands, as to the Lord. For the husband is the head of the wife as Christ is the head of the church, his body, and is himself its Savior. As the church is subject to Christ, so let wives also be subject in everything to their husbands." Col. 2:10, "And you have come to fulness of life in him, who is the head of all rule and authority." Now this principle of the headship of Jesus Christ which is the spiritual rule of the Church is mediated into a local congregation individually. This is important. In I Peter 2:4-5 Peter tells us we are living stones, a holy priesthood, built into the house of God. The rule of Jesus Christ is mediated into the local church organization through the individual who is a living stone and who has full access to the will of God and the blessings of life through Jesus Christ. The church is not a pyramid so that the one at the top is closer to heaven and has his own pipeline to heaven. I don't have a special telephone in my office where I get God's commands. Each of you has a relationship to God through Jesus Christ, and the relationship of Jesus Christ to His Church is mediated through every life that is a member.

This is important, because it helps us to understand the next step, which is—how do we discern the will of Christ. If it is true that the individual has direct access to the will of Christ and if we pray for God's will before voting, we all should vote the same way, shouldn't we? There should never be any dissenting votes. It doesn't quite work that way. The problem is that though we are individually responsible to mediate the lordship of Jesus Christ, this has to be mutually discerned, and there has to be a corrective of our own distortions, because we are not completely free agents of God, simply delivering God's message. We have our own built-in distortions, and these must be cleansed and corrected by mutual discernment, and this is why Paul said in Eph. 5:21, "Be subject to one another." If we sat here claiming the prerogative that everything we thought of was infallibly inspired by God, it would be chaos; and if every time there is a committee or a board meeting someone sits back and says—well, this is what I think and this is God's will, either accept it or not—you have chaos or fragmentation. No, we are to be subject to one another, and we are to recognize that if we have a difference of opinion, is it possible that both are inspired by God? At least we never dare say that all who disagree are wrong. We are to be subject one to another. This makes for some interesting possibilities.

Let us move from the spiritual rule of the Church, which is the headship of Jesus Christ, into the practical regulation of the church. Here we are going to discuss, first of all, the need for self-government. Turn to Acts 6 and we will see how out of the need for government in a church there arose the election of church officers. "Now in those days when the disciples were increasing in number, the Hellenists (that is, the Greek-speaking Christians) murmured against the Hebrews (that is, the Hebrew-speaking Christians) because their widows were neglected in the daily distribution." Now there were far more Hebrew-speaking Christians in the church at Jerusalem obviously than there were Greek-speaking Christians, so the Greek-speaking Christians were in the minority. They said—look, our widows are not being fed. Putting it rather plainly, they were saying—we are being discriminated against because we are fewer in number. Now verse 2, "And the twelve summoned the body of the disciples and said, 'It is not right that we should give up preaching the word of God to serve tables. Therefore, brethren, pick out from among you seven men of good repute, full of the Spirit and of wisdom, whom we may appoint to this duty' ".

Here is an interesting thing. When it comes to the practical regulation of the church, one of the first things we learn is that the church itself is responsible for this. The twelve apostles could have come in, and Peter could have made short work of this. He could have said—all right, you fellows, get in line. This is how it is going to be, and you are going to accept it. He did nothing of the kind. They said—now choose from among yourselves your own leaders to take care of this problem, and after you have chosen them, we will appoint them. This is how it works. We elect officers in this church and we have an installation service, and we recognize that though we have chosen the officers it is God who invests them with His blessing. God appoints whom we choose if we choose in His will, and it's a wonderful working together. The need for self-government is there because the church is forced to discern in a practical way what God's will is for the members.

It is interesting to note here how they solved this. Here you have a group who is going to elect a board of deacons with the first thing on the agenda to solve this problem of discrimination. Now who do they elect? Read through the list of names—you find names like Stephen, Philip, Prochorus, Nicanor, Timon, Nicolaus—not a Hebrew name in the group. Seven men were chosen from among the minority by the majority to settle this dispute. By placing responsibility upon those who have discerned the problem, they demonstrated the true spirit of recognition; they were being subject to one another. They did not use their majority rule to over-rule, and these seven men full of the Holy Spirit solved this problem because they were chosen in Christian spirit from among the group.

Is a majority decision always God's will in the practical outworking of church government? Is the church a democracy? We have claimed the congregational form of government; we have claimed for ourselves the right to decide our own affairs. Does this make us a democracy? Not one bit, for in a democracy the authority is vested in the people, is that not right? And where is the authority vested in a church? In Jesus Christ. We have chosen the democratic process as the best tool for discerning the will of Jesus Christ through mutual subjection. The authority of the church is not vested in the people but in Jesus Christ. This is not a democratic form of government, it is a monarchy, and Jesus Christ is the king.

Now then, lest you misunderstand, there are at least three major forms of church government. All three of these forms of church government, as far as I can discern, recognize this basic principle, that the authority of the church is vested in Jesus Christ. This makes all three forms of church government at least possible and not against the scriptures. All that the Bible requires is that the authority of the church be vested in Jesus Christ.

You have first as a major category the episcopal form of church government in which the bishop is the one who mediates this authority of Jesus Christ in the church. You have, secondly, the presbyterial form of government in which elected representatives, once they are elected, mediate the authority of Jesus Christ in the church; and you have the congregational form of government in which the authority of Jesus Christ is mediated through the individual members. In all three cases it is the authority of Christ that has the final word, and it is only the question of *how* the authority of Christ is mediated into a concrete situation. We choose the congregational form of government because we believe this leads us closer to the perfect working of Christ through the body of Christ. We do not claim that the congregational form of government is the only form authorized by Scripture. We only say that any form of government must recognize this, that Jesus Christ has the authority for the Church.

There is not only need for self-government, there is need for self-discipline; and we will only touch upon this. In I Cor. 5 and 6 we have some examples of this. Paul speaks to the Corinthian church and says—listen, when you have problems, why don't you settle them yourself. I find believers going to unbelievers to have them settle their problems. Aren't you mature enough to arbitrate your problems?

The church is responsible for its own self-discipline. In chapter 5, speaking of a moral problem in the church, Paul says, listen, you take care of this, this is your responsibility. But then he added an interesting footnote and clarified one thing for us, and that is that the church has no right to discipline the world, which is good for us to know. In chapter 5, verse 12, Paul says, "For what have I to do with judging outsiders? Is it not those inside the church whom you are to judge? God judges those outside. Drive out the wicked person from among you."

We are seeing far too much of the church seeking to impose a Christian ethic on the world. I talked to a minister who came from Washington. He was telling me about the effective ministerial group they had up there, and he said, "We closed down all the stores on Sunday." I was unimpressed. Now I'm not in favor of having Sunday become a commercial day, but I'm also not in favor of trying to make the world live like Christians. Why should we expect them to? We have no business to judge those outside and impose upon them the Christian ethic—they're not Christians. He told me they had one fellow in a large chain super-market who didn't want to close his store because, he said—my best customers arrive after twelve o'clock when church is out, and I think you're looking in the wrong place for the problem if you have one. I think he was right. Paul said—what have I to do with judging outsiders? A pastor in a nearby church told me their ministerial group put on enough pressure to close all the real estate offices in their community on Sunday, and he said—we started to work on the car dealers, but in the meantime the realtors opened up again. The authority of the church is not exercised over the world; there are some groups who misunderstand this. The authority of Jesus Christ is mediated through the members and to each other to form the church—a disciplined community.

There is the matter of the fraternal responsibility of the church. We have said that the local congregation is a complete manifestation of the body of Christ. Does this mean we are sufficient in ourselves? Not any more than one man is sufficient in himself. We need each other. We are all a part of humanity and a man alone is an incomplete man from the standpoint of his life—he's a complete man by definition, but not in fellowship. We need each other. Paul said in Col. 2:5, "For though I am absent in body, yet I am with you in spirit." And there is a sense of belonging to each other. Does this mean that we belong only to other Evangelical Free Churches? Not at all, for our relationship is to the body of Christ primarily. Oh, we are a household of faith—as Evangelical Free Churches we have mutual recognition of a distinctive as we carry it in common, but not for a moment are we saying that our relationship with another Evangelical Free Church is a closer relationship to the body of Christ than with another group which is a true church.

It's like your family and your neighbors, your family has a closer relationship than your neighbors do to you, but as far as humanity is concerned they are all persons. Just because members of your family are closer doesn't make them more human, does it? (I know what you're thinking—more inhuman!) The point is that we are a complete church and yet not sufficient of ourselves, because we need each other. We need to reach out and share, and as an Evangelical Free Church we have mutual recognition with other Evangelical Free Churches of these distinctives, but we have fellowship with every local congregation in this community who believe that Jesus Christ is the head of the Church and which is composed of those who are born again into His fellowship.

Take this thought with you. "For in him the whole fulness of deity dwells bodily, and you have come to fulness of life in him" (Col. 2:9-10). This is marvelous, that in Jesus Christ all of the divinity of God was focused. He was complete God and in Him, in Jesus Christ, we are complete man, and we have come to fullness of life in Him. Is this not why we seek mutual fellowship? We need each other—we recognize we are incomplete by ourselves and so we seek mutual completeness in the body of Christ. But we recognize that mutual fellowship is not sufficient of itself. There are many clubs and organizations which try this, but in our mutual fellowship through Jesus Christ we are complete in Him and have come to fullness of life in Him.

Is your life full? I don't mean full of busy things to do—I mean, is your life full of happiness and joy and peace and value? Is it? If not, then you belong in fellowship seeking this fullness in Jesus Christ. This is why we are here—we are seeking as individuals to draw from the fullness that Christ is so that we might become mature and full and growing. Come and grow with us, come to the place where we all find an inexhaustible source of forgiveness and mercy and love and inspiration. Come—because you cannot live alone.

ARTICLE XI

We believe in the personal premillennial and imminent coming of our Lord Jesus Christ and that this "blessed hope" has a vital bearing on the personal life and service of the believer.

CHAPTER ELEVEN

OUR BLESSED HOPE

There is no doctrine of the Church which has provoked more controversy than the second coming of Jesus Christ; in fact, because of the weird speculations and the improbable conclusions, many Christians are embarrassed that we should even have to discuss it. We make no apology for believing in the second coming of Jesus Christ, nor do we avoid discussion of it, and it is fitting that it is included in our Statement of Faith.

There are several passages of Scripture, extended passages, that deal with the second coming of Christ. Several hundred passages point to this truth either directly or by inference, and it is important for us to understand that in each of these major portions the context in which the Scripture discusses the second coming of Christ is one of immediate personal crisis. This is true of Matthew 24 and the parallel passages in Mark 12 and Luke 21. Here the immediate personal crisis was the impending death of Jesus Christ and the insecurity of the disciples. In this dramatic crisis Jesus gave them the teaching concerning the relationship of His ministry to their faith and the end of the age. In I Thessaloinans 4, another passage of Scripture that deals extensively with this truth, we have the immediate personal crisis in this new church produced by the death of Christian believers. Some who had laid to rest husbands and wives, friends, and sons and daughters, were unsure that their faith was real enough to stand in the face of death. Into this personal crisis of anxiety the apostle Paul taught them the security of one who had been loved of God, and the evidence of this security is that Jesus Christ Himself shall some day come and reunite those who still live and those who have gone before. For in Christ death has lost its power of separation. In II Thess. 2, in the confusion produced by false teachers who were teaching that the day of the Lord had already come, the apostle Paul once more taught further truth concerning the day of the Lord. To take passages of Scripture dealing with the second coming of Christ and to use them as proof texts for any particular doctrine and to ignore the existential crisis involved in their first deliverance is not only to distort the truth but to make it highly irrelevant, and there is no greater distortion of God's Word than to discuss it with irrelevance.

It is important as we discuss this basic truth of our church and of God's Word that we understand first of all the concept of eschatology and the true Biblical basis of eschatology. The word "eschatology" is rather foreign and forbidding, I know, but it has an honest heritage. The word is derived from the Greek word *eskatos* which simply means last or the final number in a sequence. So eschatology is simply the doctrine of last things, the doctrine of ultimate issues; and in this sense it is important for us to understand that life demands an eschatology. Your life demands it, and mine does. You cannot live without some firm conviction in the reality of ultimate issues, at least as far as you are concerned. Life will quickly become impossible and futile if you do not have an eschatology, which is to say, if you do not have an ultimate meaning and purpose.

This week I talked and prayed with a woman who was suffering intense pain. She had been suffering this pain for several weeks and it had reached the place where the pain had become unreasonable and impossible. She was on the brink of despair and loss of self-control and needed not so much to be relieved of the pain as to be reassured that there was sense to this unreasonable pain. Her opening words were not—I am in pain—but—I am afraid—for fear is a greater reality than pain. Pain is only a circumstance, and fear is honest reality. In our discussion we did not discuss the symptomology of pain, nor did we discuss any quick promise as to the alleviation of pain, but we discussed in the midst of pain a deep and abiding purpose to life that would give sense through pain until she could find an eschatology for her pain and her life, until she could know without a shadow of doubt that God had determined from the beginning that there should be an end.

If somehow we feel that we are cast adrift in this universe with a beginning and no end, there is not one of us who can bear it. Life demands an eschatology, demands a sensible end, a meaningful conclusion to that which has already begun. In this sense history demands an eschatology, because history is only the experience of man, and history without eschatology is chaos. This is why we have a right to believe not only in the eschatology of God's will and redemptive love, but in the eschatology that reaches and encompasses the entire history of man and the world.

The day of the Lord is not a novelty in the New Testament. The Old Testament must be understood in the context of a redemptive historical work of God, that whenever God moved into the history of man He moved with redemptive love. He chose His people in Egypt and delivered them through Moses; He followed His people through the wilderness and led them into the promised land; He delivered them in extremity; He provided kings to govern them; He sent prophets to witness to them of God's truth, and even in exile He recovered His people and rebuilt for them a sanctuary. God's redemptive love always has an historical framework, and God's design has always been to work through the history of man in bringing to consummation the idea that He had before the creation of the world. If you are to understand the significance of the word "eschatology" you must understand that we are not looking at life from the beginning to the end, but we are looking at life from the end back towards the beginning; that we are speaking not so much of what we hope shall be or what might be, but we speak of what already is in the mind of God and towards that reality the history of man is inevitably moving.

The Old Testament speaks of the redemptive community as being a geographic and national entity. But in the Old Testament the relationship between the kingdom of God and the world which was its environment was imperfect, and because of this the people of God suffered oppression and were dominated by forces without and within. In the midst of this community of God's people there was a great cry and a great promise of salvation, and this promise of deliverance and salvation took the form of a future day of the Lord—a day in which God would rescue His people from their oppression; He would deliver them from the heavy hand of the intruder; He would save them from their own sins and shame. Throughout the Old Testament we have this building expectation of the day of the Lord—O God, when shall that day come. O God, when shall you come to restore order to this world—when will you come to justify the righteous and judge the wicked.

It would be well for us to look at several passages in the book of Isaiah to gain an insight into this great expectation of the day of the Lord. "For the Lord of hosts has a day against all that is proud and lofty, against all that is lifted up and high" (Isa. 2:12). It goes on in the next few verses to describe the effects of the day against the wicked, those who have oppressed God's people. In another passage, "In that day the branch of the Lord shall be beautiful and glorious, and the fruit of the land shall be the pride and glory of the survivors of Israel" (Isa. 4:2). Here that day is a day of prosperity and well-being for God's people. Isa. 11:6-9 speaks of the transformed creation where the earth itself shall be a testimony to the transforming power of God. "The wolf shall dwell with the lamb, and the leopard shall lie down with the kid, and the calf and the lion and the fatling together, and a little child shall lead them. The cow and the bear shall feed; their young shall lead them. The and the lion shall eat straw like the ox." Figurative language, picturing for us that in that day there shall be a restoration of the harmony of all creation. Creation shall not ravage itself against its own kind. In Isa. 11:1-5, "There shall come forth a shoot from the stump of Jesse, and a branch shall grow out of hs roots. And the Spirit of the Lord shall rest upon him, the spirit of wisdom and understanding . . ." In Joel 3 we have portrayed that terrible day of vengence, the day of darkness, the day of wrath. Through the entire Old Testament we have this growing expectation of the day of the Lord.

Now into this environment came Jesus, and Jesus acknowledged the fact that He was truly the Messiah, so in the New Testament we have a strange mystery concerning the day of the Lord. In Acts 2:16 on the day of Pentecost Peter arose and said—the day has come. He points back to the prophet Joel and says, "This is the day of which Joel spoke, the day of the Lord is here." He quotes Joel, "In the last day I will pour out my spirit on all flesh, your sons and your daughters shall prophesy, your old men shall dream dreams." The day of the Lord is here, Peter said, this is the day of God's sovereign movement. And yet something's wrong because this is not a day of vengence. Jesus did not come with a sword in His hand to slay the wicked; Jesus came as a shoot out of dry ground; He came as a gentle Savior who bore the scorn and ridicule of all men and who was so weak in His helpless love that He could not defend Himself and He died upon the cross. So the day of the Lord had come, and yet it is still to come, as Paul makes clear in I Thessalonians 4 and II Thessalonians 2. Now how are we to understand this?

It must be pictured for us that in our present age there is an overlapping of the age which is yet to come and the age which now is. As far as the Old Testament is concerned, these ages are on a straight line, and when the end of the age that now is came everyone would be in the age which is to come and we would have the millenium, and the lion would lie down with the lamb. But when Jesus came He introduced the new age, and yet history continues its course. Sin is not completely destroyed though it has ultimately been forgiven on the cross, and so we have an overlapping. The age which is to come has now entered into this age and overlaps it. In this period, this interim period of which the New Testament speaks as the "last days", we have all of the blessings of the age which is to come in terms of justification, redemption, forgiveness of sin, eternal life, all of the fruits of the Spirit, every assurance of heaven's joy. All of these are presently available to us in Jesus Christ, almost as if Jesus Christ in descending to us is a channel through which all of eternity has poured. And yet there is a strange period of time in which history still labors on, almost in its death movements, during which time the kingdom of God and the kingdom of this world are locked in mortal conflict, and the children of light live amid the children of darkness. These are the last days, and Jesus Christ is the dividing line between the age to come and the age which now is.

Understanding that this is the eschatological framework of the Bible, that through Jesus Christ the age which is to come is now here, we can draw certain conclusions which are drawn forth for us in our Statement of Faith. First of all, the day of the Lord has an *imminent consummation,* and this is because it has already begun. Now that which has begun needs no signs of its beginning, and that which is imminent needs no signs of its conclusion, and this is why the word "imminent" is used— not because something is about to begin, but because something has already begun and is about to be finished. Though we have almost 2,000 years of history in this interim, in God's time table this is one day—the day of the Lord. Though we stretch that day with our chronology, as far as God's redemptive purpose is concerned it is one day, one event, the coming of Jesus Christ which has two historical foci, His first coming and His second coming. The day of the Lord has an imminent consummation because it has already begun and only waits consummation.

Now there are certain attitudes that this imminence ought to provoke. Matthew 24: 36-44, "But of the day and hour no one knows, not even the angels in heaven nor the Son but the Father only." Jesus goes on to portray for us the attitude that one should have in the light of this imminent conclusion, and that is that we ought not to predict the end of something that has already begun. Jesus said—even the Son does not know. Now here is where there has been much speculation concerning the coming of Jesus Christ. It is wrong to anticipate it and cease working. This was the problem in the church at Thessalonica. We read of this in II Thess. 3:6-11. Paul has to rebuke them for this mistake. Here Paul speaks of the wrong attitude of imminence. "Now we command you, brethren, in the name of our Lord Jesus Christ, that you keep away from any brother who is living in idleness and not in accord with the tradition that you received from us. For you yourselves know how you ought to imitate us; we were not idle when we were with you, we did not eat any one's bread without paying, but with toil and labor we worked night and day, that we might not burden any of you." Verse 11, "For we hear that some of you are living in idleness, mere busybodies, not doing any work. Now such persons we command and exhort in the Lord Jesus Christ to do their work in quietness and to earn their own living."

If I were absolutely sure that the day of the Lord was about to reach its consummation, I would not waste my time in working for the future. I would not paint the walls of my home, I would not water the grass that tomorrow I shall not see, so idleness could very well be taken as a spiritual attitude of faith, and this is what the Thessalonians were doing. Paul said—this is the wrong attitude of imminence, for you do not know when the day of the Lord shall come. Thus you must live as though your life is going to be going on.

There is a counterpart to this failure, and this is found

in Luke 21:34-36. Here there were some who said—well, life has been going on and it will go on. "But take heed to yourselves lest your hearts be weighted down with dissipation and drunkenness and cares of this life, and that day come upon you suddenly like a snare." There is only one explanation as to how we are to live. We are to live in such a way that we shall never be taken by surprise but that we shall always have something to do tomorrow. This is the true attitude of faith. The day of the Lord has an imminent consummation—it is about to conclude and has been about to conclude for the last 2000 years.

The day of the Lord also has an *historical consequence*. It is not simply a spiritual attitude. Rev. 1:7 says every eye will see Him when He comes—the whole world will see Him. Acts 1:11 says that the same Jesus who lived here shall come again. In Matthew 24 Jesus says that every tribe of earth shall see Him. II Peter 3:10 tells us the elements of this universe shall be dissolved with fiery heat. The day of the Lord shall have an historical consequence.

The most important thing about the day of the Lord is that it has a *personal implication*. This we read in II Peter 3:11, "Since all these things are thus to be dissolved, what sort of persons ought you to be in lives of holiness and godliness, waiting for and hastening the coming of the day of God, because of which the heavens will be kindled and dissolved, and the elements will melt with fire! But according to his promise we wait for new heavens and a new earth in which righteousness dwells." It would be very easy for us to reassure ourselves that we hold to the orthodox interpretation of the second coming of Jesus Christ and to walk out of here saying—it is fine to believe it— and yet to have missed the whole point. For if He has not come for you, He shall not come again—not really— because it's the same Jesus who is coming, not a different one. This means that this doctrine first of all calls us back to the fact that Jesus has already come, and that in His second coming He will add nothing that has not already been said.

Do you wait for a new basis of reconciliation with God?

Then you wait in vain. Do you wait for a new place of beginning where you can become honest with yourself? Then you wait in vain. Do you wait for new wisdom that makes eternal life more reasonable? Then you wait in vain. Do you wait for answers to problems that are yet unsolved? Then you wait in vain. He will bring no answers, He will bring no wisdom, He will bring no love, He will bring no life, He will bring no peace, He will bring no happiness, He will bring no joy—we are supposed to *have* all this; and if you don't have it, He has nothing for you; and if *this* moment isn't worth anything to you, eternity will be worth nothing. He has nothing to make your life worthwhile if you cannot bear it now. What more can God say to us other than the words of love that He died for us, in order that we may become through Him who we were meant to be.

I fear that many of us wait for the second coming of Jesus Christ as if somehow there is a large bank account for us and it's all going to be delivered to us on that day. I assure you that on that day God is only going to confirm for us what we already have. I dare to believe that all that I shall ever have in eternity is real to me right now. I hold on to that by faith and it's a precarious thing because my own body, even my own heart, would let it slip away, but I hold on to it by faith, and I believe that through Jesus Christ I have all of the happiness and joy that God meant for me. The second coming of Jesus Christ for me will simply be the confirmation of this present intimation, and I long for that. I long for that because I spend many moments in darkness. I have moments in which my faith seems to have eluded me, and so I long for that moment in which there shall be no more hindrance to expression, but I do not ask for greater expression than He's already given me. I do not ask for greater joy, I only ask that the frustrations be removed—and they will. I do not ask that He give me greater joy than the joy I've had through tears—I only ask that He shall wipe the tears away Himself. I do not ask that He prove anything by destroying the world—I only ask that He conserve everything He's already given to me. Why do you wait for the second coming? In some expectation of something that you do not have? Then you wait in vain. Jesus Christ has already come, and the same Jesus will come again. The point is—will He know you?

ARTICLE XII

We believe in the bodily resurrection of the dead; of the believer to everlasting blessedness and joy with the Lord, of the unbeliever to judgment and everlasting conscious punishment.

CHAPTER TWELVE

OUR GLORIOUS HERITAGE

Our age has made its peace with time and chance. It has quickly settled with the uncertainty of death and has chosen to make this life of highest value. The tragic thing of our age is not its self-deception but its sophistication in which it is willing to sacrifice the intimations of the heart for the bread of immediate life. We find men today who are willing to sacrifice belief in eternal life and in future life for the individual for the impersonal existence of ideas and truth itself, as if there would be any truth without life. What a tragedy it is when a principle such as justice has greater value than the existence of one human soul; for if the grave is the end of human life, then there is no justice.

Let it be understood that the resurrection is not an optional doctrine of Christianity. There would be no definition of the word without Jesus Christ. There would only be the vague intimation that there ought to be something, but there would be no definition of what that something is, except that Jesus Christ has already been resurrected from the dead. Let it be understood that we speak not *of* His resurrection. We speak *because* of His resurrection of our own. We speak of the truth of who we are and who we shall be, knowing that until we have spoken of that truth, we have a lingering fear in our heart that shall discourage us from seeking the best in life. Nor do we speak of simply restoration to life, of which we have many examples in Scripture. If all we have to look forward to is the experience of Lazarus who was called forth out of the grave to die again, we have little improvement over our first venture. No, we speak of a new creation; we speak of something that no man has ever experienced except the man Jesus Christ in whose likeness we seek to find our own.

When we speak of the resurrection of the dead, we must affirm first of all that death is an indignity, that death has no right to be accepted as the final value in life. There is no such thing as noble death. It is always ignoble, and no matter how courageous, no matter how heroic the spirit, death is always the final indignity. This is why it is so important that we are able to find some dignity in death, for if we find no dignity in death there is no dignity in life; and all of the heroism and all of the courage of man is simply a brave attempt to bluff his own heart and to get through the existence of time. We would do well to raise a protest against the indignity of death. We would do well to reverse the course of our age and to cry out that death itself must be answered and that all of the technology of our age and all of the scientific thought and all of the philosophy of our age is insufficient in light of the indignity of death.

We turn to the Old Testament and find the first intimation that death is an indignity and has no right over the personality. In the book of Job, chapter 14, a man who was forced by his circumstances of darkness to discover the possibility of light looked deep within his own heart and dared to say some things that as yet had no validation in history. He said with his heart what Jesus Christ later was to reenact, that we all might have assurance. Job said, "For there is hope for a tree, if it be cut down, that it will sprout again, and that its shoots will not cease. Though its roots grow old in the earth, and its stump die in the ground, yet at the scent of water it will bud and put forth branches like a young plant. But man dies, and is laid low; man breathes his last, and where is he? As waters fail from a lake, and a river wastes away and dries up, so man lies down and rises not again" (Job 14:7-12).

You see, the argument of Job was that even a tree buds again, even a tree that dies in the winter has a Spring, even the barrenness of that dark, cold ground carries within it the germ of life that only needs the scent of water and the fragrance of warmth to bud. But, he said, man is placed in the earth, and where is he? In the 19th chapter Job once more at the extremity of his darkness reached down in his heart and said more—"I know that my Redeemer lives, and at last he will stand upon the earth; and after my skin has been thus destroyed, then from my flesh I shall see God, whom I shall see on my side, and my eyes shall behold and not another." If a man die, shall he live again? said Job. And he insisted—if he doesn't, he ought to, because a tree does. What a miscarriage of justice this is if man can think of his own future and yet not have it, but a tree which cannot think of its own presence yet has a future. The logic of the heart refuses to accept the indignity of death. If death is not a portal to a greater life, then this life is an indignity.

Think of Jesus who refused to accept death. He did not try to fool himself by saying that death is not real—He simply refused to accept it as final. Every funeral service He attended He broke up with a restoration to life, and His own tears were affirmation of the fact that death had no right of existence, and He wept and groaned because He saw the indignity of death. We must once more raise a protest against the value of death—it is an ignoble thing, and we must lead forth the heart once more to ask the question—what is there in life that can cancel out the indignity of death?

Our Statement of Faith speaks of the bodily resurrection, and it affirms the fact that death is an indignity, but it goes further than that and affirms the fact that life itself is eternal, not just that the spirit is eternal, for life is the history of the spirit in the existence of time. Why care about the body, anyway—it's such a burden. Why is it that we have taken the position in our Statement of Faith that we believe in a bodily resurrection and not just in immortality of the spirit and soul? We carry around with us this body which is a frustration of the spirit, a hindrance to the intimations of the heart, a symbol of deterioration that begins with the moment of birth, and we labor all of our days with cosmetics and technique to delay the inevitable. Let's face it—we are falling apart. We are decaying, we are facing a losing struggle that somehow we must make the flesh live longer than its appointed day. There comes a time when we give up the struggle and accept the inevitable, and then there comes a time when we long for freedom from the body. There comes a weariness to the spirit when the body refuses to participate in even the minimal joys of life, when the body becomes only a center of pain and an ignoble thing itself.

Why care about the body—why not look upon the resurrection as one last glorious freedom from the body? Because the body is the embodiment of life and spirit. The body is not simply flesh and blood, the body is the place in the universe for the human spirit to dwell; the body is the embodiment of personality; it is the history of the human soul. For it is with the body that we move and express ourselves in time, and every bit of our expression is the history of the spirit, and do you not care for the history of the spirit? Do you not care a little bit about the continuing presence of who you are? Ah, we care about the body because we cherish the life of the spirit.

Paul said in II Cor. 5:4—it's not that we desire to be unclothed, but that we might be clothed further. We don't desire that we should become some vague spirit in an ambiguous spiritual world—we want a place in heaven; we want a place in God's presence, not just to be a part of His personality. So that the bodily resurrection is the assurance to the individual that this history of who he is shall not be lost, the assurance that the touch in time is preserved eternally. It's the assurance that all of our movement which has been before God is now preserved in the history of who we are. The body is not just a temporary tool of the spirit, the body is not just a memento of something that once was; the body is the arena of life itself being lived, and that which is lived is eternal. *Life* is eternal, not the future. Life itself, the history of the self, is eternal, and that which is enacted in time shall never be lost, and the resurrection of the body is the assurance that all of the realities of this life are eternal realities. We brush against one another in the darkness of the world, we scarcely know what we do, some of those movements are tentative, some of those movements are planned, some of those movements are rare moments in which we recognize each other and speak a word of recognition. The resurrection of the body means that those moments shall not be lost, and those moments of recognition are part of the history of who we are, and the resurrection is continuity of life because life is eternal. How difficult for us to understand this. We think of life as being entirely temporal and the future as eternal.

Some ask and rightly so—if the body is so important and is the history of the spirit, what then is the resurrection body like? We have not been the first to ask that question, nor shall we be the last. The apostle Paul faced this problem in I Cor. 15:35, "But some one will ask, 'How are the dead raised? With what kind of body do they come?'" And Paul rebukes the question just a little bit and says, "You foolish man! What you sow does not come to life unless it dies, and what you sow is not the body which is to be, but a bare kernel, perhaps of wheat or of some other grain. But God gives it a body as he has chosen, and to each kind of seed its own body." He goes on in verse 42, "So is it with the resurrection of the dead. What is sown is perishable, what is raised is imperishable. It is sown in dishonor, it is raised in glory. It is sown in weakness, it is raised in power. It is sown a physical body, it is raised a spiritual body. If there is a physical body, there is also a spiritual body." The physical body is only the shadow of the spiritual. We are not moving from the physical to an indefinite spiritual being, but we have first the reality of the spiritual body, and the physical body is only a faint reflection of this suited to temporal life. The resurrection body is imperishable, it is not flesh and blood.

The new body is a personal one. You will note in verse 38, "God gives it a body as he has chosen, and to each kind of seed its own body." I don't know what the connection is between our bodies here on earth and our resurrection bodies. The Scripture says out of the dust we shall be raised and given a body again, and yet the particles of the dust that make up my physical body are perishable. Is there a germ of the body in the spirit? Like the germ of the flower in the seed, so that even if all of the elements which comprise our physical body were dissolved, there is nonetheless a profile which shall carve out its own likeness in whatever substance it be? God shall take spiritual substance and shall not need again to fashion the likeness of a body, for we have our own profile, and all we need is spiritual substance. Somewhere within the power of the spirit itself, created in the image of God, there is the profile of a personal body. Yes, you will recognize yourself and others in heaven. You will have a personal being, a personal body.

Our Statement of Faith affirms the indignity of death in order that life may have dignity. It affirms that life is eternal in order that the history of the self may not be lost; but most important, it affirms this, that the individual is immortal. The uniqueness of personhood transcends time, and if you would mark one difference in the ultimate of Christianity and the ultimate of all other world religions and irreligion itself, it would be that Christianity requires the uniqueness of the personality over and above time and death.

A quotation from the Soviet Encyclopedia, 1929, reveals the other alternative: "This dogma (that is, the dogma of the resurrection) is found to be in the most decisive contradiction with scientific natural knowledge which confesses the inescapability of death as the destruction of individuality with its physical psychical peculiarities." The inescapability of death as the destruction of individuality! If you're looking for the one distinctive of atheistic communism, it is this absolute belief in the destruction of individuality. If you believe in the destruction of the individuality at death, you are forced to devaluate the individual in life and to give your highest value to ideas, and especially ideas which are temporal.

Immortality is a present dignity. Take a beautiful flower which has reached the ultimate of its perfection, has extended its passion of beauty into fragrance and color; but then watch that flower die and know that in the dying of the flower is the extinction of its being. The flower has never been, once it has died, because the flower has no remembrance of itself. But give the flower immortality, and instead of at the moment of death the petals falling to the ground, the fragrance drying up and disappearing and the color fading out, give that flower at its finest perfection immortality—and what a difference there is! Then the flower always shall be at its finest. Now do one more thing—give the flower knowledge of this while it still lives, and what a difference it makes! So that as the flower is buffeted by circumstances, the wind, the sand, and the darkness, as the flower pushes its precarious beauty up into an alien world and is decapitated, give the flower knowledge that it is immortal and you shall see the reality of hope and faith in existence. Immortality is the dignity of existence, it enables us to push the feeble faith that we are more than creatures in time up into an alien world and to know that we have an existence that trenscends time. But death is no friend of unbelief, no comfort to the lost, for the individual is immortal.

In the book of Daniel, chapter 12, there is an inescapable reality. "Many of those who lie in the dust of the earth shall awake, some to everlasting life and some to shame and everlasting contempt." It is inescapable, the individual is immortal, the individual cannot be extinguished. Once given an existence, that existence cannot be blown out. Thus we believe in the bodily resurrection of everyone. We believe in a bodily existence in a spiritual world for every created human being. To some it will be the fulfillment of every joy, every longing, every need, and every desire. For some it will be the consignment to loneliness without hope, a wandering not as a disembodied spirit but the wandering of one who has a body but no fellowship, who has being but no expression, who has the capacity to love but now no one to love and no place to love.

We believe in the immortality of the individual, a bodily resurrection which to those who have found through faith in Jesus Christ a place in God's redemptive love, joy and blessedness; but to those who persist in being lost, a spitual existence in bodily form of eternal lostness. We would rather not believe this, if it were ours to choose. Apparently God had no choice, that immortality is itself, and once created He cannot reclaim it. Apparently God cut off a portion of His own being and sent it into the universe, not in a temporary existence but in an eternal one, and if it is to be eternally estranged, there is nothing God can do about it because immortality is itself. Why did He take that risk? Because He desired the destruction of the lost? No, because He desired the love of those who are found. He desired someone to love Him. He desired someone who could eternally exist with Him and express this love through their own personality. Too great a risk, you say? No, because life is the fullness of God Himself. He could do nothing else.

We believe in the bodily resurrection of the dead. To you who believe, it is the assurance of your immortality, and you can face death with dignity because death is only a portal to the fullness of who you are with God. If there are those of you who have no relationship with God, you ought to know that you are immortal. We cannot do any more for you than to remind you that you are immortal, and to remind you that the only cure for being eternally lost is to be eternally saved. We are not so interested in having you confess your sins in order that you might find a measure of status with us—I trust we are not so insecure that we need that. But you are immortal, and immortally—who are you?

www.ingramcontent.com/pod-product-compliance
Lightning Source LLC
Chambersburg PA
CBHW050838160426
43192CB00011B/2071